Deifying Vision

Deifying Vision

Reclaiming an Anagogical Imagination

James McCullough

FOREWORD BY
Philip Krill

CASCADE *Books* • Eugene, Oregon

DEIFYING VISION
Reclaiming an Anagogical Imagination

Cascade Books
An Imprint of Wipf and Stock Publishers
199 W. 8th Ave., Suite 3
Eugene, OR 97401

www.wipfandstock.com

PAPERBACK ISBN: 979-8-3852-2905-5
HARDCOVER ISBN: 979-8-3852-2906-2
EBOOK ISBN: 979-8-3852-2907-9

Cataloguing-in-Publication data:

Names: McCullough, James [author]. | Krill, Philip [foreword writer]

Title: Deifying vision : reclaiming an anagogical imagination / by James Mc-Cullough ; foreword by Philip Krill.

Description: Eugene, OR: Cascade Books, 2025 | Includes bibliographical references and index.

Identifiers: ISBN 979-8-3852-2905-5 (paperback) | ISBN 979-8-3852-2906-2 (hardcover) | ISBN 979-8-3852-2907-9 (ebook)

Subjects: LCSH: Spiritual life—Christianity. | Bible.—Criticism, interpretation, etc. | Deification (Christianity). | Mysticism. | Trinity.

Classification: BS617 M33 2025 (paperback) | BS617 (ebook)

VERSION NUMBER 02/05/25

To Fr. Philip Krill

Ever promoting a Trinitarian vision of deification
and contemplative prayer

Trinity!! Higher than any being,
        any divinity, any goodness!
    Guide of Christians
        in the wisdom of heaven!
Lead us up beyond unknowing and light,
    up to the farthest, highest peak
        of mystic Scripture,
    where the mysteries of God's Word
        lie simple, absolute and unchangeable
        in the brilliant darkness of a hidden silence.[1]

Ascent (*anabasis*) or anagogy (*anagoge*) is the purpose not only of exegesis, but of all of life, since it is through ascent or anagogy that one increasingly participates in the heavenly or eschatological reality of the divine life.[2]

What is the *Totus Christus* other than the final, full participation of humanity in the *perichoresis* of the Trinity? Can the fullness of Trinitarian glory be realized without God, in Christ, "drawing all things to himself" (John 12:32) so he can be "all in all" (I Cor 15:28)?[3]

1. Pseudo-Dionysius, "The Mystical Theology," from *The Complete Works*, 135.

2. Boersma, *Embodiment and Virtue in Gregory of Nyssa*, 3.

3. Krill, *Aporiae*, 41.

Contents

Foreword

MY LIFE FOUND ITS inherent purpose when, in 1994, while teaching the freshly minted *Catechism of the Catholic Church*, a student drew my attention to a statement of St. Athanasius: "God became man so man could become God" (CCC 460). The student believed this to be heretical, since "man becoming God" (without qualification) seemed to him completely foreign to his previous catechetical formation and fully at odds with the theory of atonement he had learned in Catholic grade school. Having myself never encountered this quote, I was likewise incredulous. How could it be that Christ's *kenosis* (his becoming man, as St. Paul describes it in Phil 2) could be our *theosis* (the patristic term for "becoming God")? How could the whole of creation be definitively redeemed simply by the Divine Word assuming our humanity in the womb of Mary? It seemed too wild to be intelligible. It seemed frankly too good to be true. And imagine my surprise when I discovered that not only did St. Athanasius say what the *Catechism* said he said, but so also did virtually every other Church Father, from Origen of Alexandria and St. Irenaeus of Lyons to St. John of Damascus and St. Maximus the Confessor.

Following this initial shock, I spent the next twenty-five years immersed in the patristic vision of deification as the purpose of the incarnation. From this immersion came my first book, *Life in the Trinity: A Catholic Vision of Communion and Deification.* Self-published and unpurchased, this book, and the vision it hoped to promote, lay like an undigested diamond the belly of the local church where I serve as a Catholic priest. Meanwhile a colleague on the faculty of the diaconate formation program in our diocese, Dr. James McCullough, noticed an inconspicuous signature tagline on an email I sent to my students in a course I was teaching on the Trinity. The line read: "Promoting a Trinitarian vision of deification and contemplative prayer." Having caught his eye, Dr. McCullough contacted me, and we had a series of conversations that resulted in a new version of *Life in the Trinity*—a collaborative effort between Dr. McCullough and myself, subsequently published by Wipf and Stock.

In this present book, Dr. McCullough explores the anagogical hermeneutic that underlies a deified vision of the Christian life. We don't need Steven Covey to remind us to "begin with the end in mind," nor Rick Warren to imagine "the purpose-driven life"; the early Church, beginning with Origen of Alexandria and St. Irenaeus of Lyons and St. John of Damascus and Maximus the Confessor and many others, approached Scripture, tradition, and the mystery of Christ with exactly these two interpretive tools. Throughout the patristic period and the high Middle Ages, a four-fold model of biblical exegesis emerged, described in meticulous detail by Henri de Lubac, in which both the mystery of Christ as God's Alpha and Omega and the biblical record concerning him is cast in a thoroughly eschatological key. With the likes of Hans Boersma, Matthew Levering, and other proponents of what has come to be known as "participative exegesis," a neo-patristic synthesis is slowly taking place, within which Dr. McCullough's book serves as a welcome addition.

Shortly before his death in 1984, the great Karl Rahner said, "The Christian of the future will be a mystic or will not exist at all." Acquiring a deified vision of the incarnation and the Christian life, inspired and supported by an anagogical approach to Scripture and tradition, is the ecclesial corollary of Rahner prophetic words.

Thankful for Jim McCullough's work and that of the editorial team at Wipf and Stock, I pray that the readers of this book will, as they ponder these pages, find themselves taken up evermore completely into the Life of the Most Holy Trinity,

Philip Krill

15 August 2024—Assumption of the Theotokos

Preface

THIS BOOK IS IN many ways a continuation of the project begun in *Life in the Trinity: The Mystery of God and Human Deification* which I coauthored with the Rev. Philip Krill. That book explores Catholic doctrine—particularly Christology—with the aim of helping Christians perceive the truth of God and the truth of themselves in relation to God, a purpose summarized as a mission to promote "a Trinitarian vision of deification and contemplative prayer." This book centers itself on a consideration of biblical hermeneutics—the ways in which Scripture is read toward that same missional end of deification and contemplative prayer. Christianity is a religion of the Word,[1] and so how the words of this Word are read and understood profoundly affects how participants understand their way of life.

The New Testament itself reflects the beginning of a uniquely Christian approach to sacred Scripture. An insistence on the reality of its portrayal of the story of Jesus grounds everything else it has to say about God and the world. At the same time, Jesus

1. "The Christian faith is not a 'religion of the book.' Christianity is the religion of the 'Word' of God, a word which is not a written and mute word, but incarnate and living." If the Scriptures are not to remain a dead letter, Christ, the eternal Word of the living God, must, through the Holy Spirit, "open [our] minds to understand the Scriptures" (CCC 108).

himself and his apostolic interpreters engage in strategies of appropriating the Scriptures of Israel within a new context. Typology, for instance, where figures and events of the Old Testament are perceived as anticipating and being fulfilled in figures and events of the New. Spiritualizing or allegorical techniques are similarly applied. Moral principles are derived from the historical past of the people of Israel, and a pervasive sense that all things aim to serve the ascension of the people of God informs the writing and self-reflection on the words of the Scripture.

Today, many readers are familiar with what is referred to as the four senses of Scripture: the literal, the allegorical, the tropological (or moral), and the anagogical.[2] This scheme is itself a kind of typology that highlights the way in which the words and intentions of Scripture exist in a multivalent, multidimensional, mutually enriching manner that, when appropriated as such, can sponsor a vision of the multivalent, multidimensional, mutually enriching dimensions of Christian experience and spirituality.

How do these four senses "work" in the interpretation and appropriation of Scripture? Consider the city of Jerusalem. Literally, it is a human dwelling place located 31°46′44″N 35°13′32″E and which served as the political and religious capital of ancient Israel. Allegorically, Jerusalem symbolizes God's presence with his people wherever they are and of their incorporation in his purposes for the world. Morally or "tropologically," Jerusalem is an image of the saintly heart, like a city with virtues that protect its innocence and integrity, the breaching or weakening of which invite apostasy and failure. Anagogically, Jerusalem is the ascended or heavenly existence of the Church, that is, of God's people in God's place in God's presence. The multivalent significance of Jerusalem is increased when one recalls that in Scripture one always approaches the city by way of ascent; one always goes "up" to Jerusalem. On one hand, one is literally going up because of the elevated terrain on which the city was founded. In a "spiritual" sense, for the faithful Israelite, approaching Jerusalem meant nearing the high place where the LORD was worshiped. Now for the Christian, going "up" to

2. See *Catechism of the Catholic Church* (CCC) 115–18.

Jerusalem is a movement of ascendance in Christ. This is the logic of the different senses of Scripture.

And so the tradition of the four senses maintains that Scripture exists with a multitude of significances which cohere around a consistent but emerging picture of God's creative and redemptive purposes for the world. Indeed, this is one of the driving motifs of this project: to alert Christians to and help them resist the tendencies of our age to *reduce* the gospel experience to a select option of just one or two emphases.

Of those four senses or levels of Scripture, most are familiar with the literal and the tropological or moral. Historical criticism, the study of Scripture that emphasizes matters of original context, intention, and transmission has done much to recover the authorial intention of the biblical writers and, from a faith perspective, how they sought to enunciate the Word of God to their generation. Likewise morally speaking, following two world wars and heightened sensitivities towards social matters, Christians became understandably concerned to practice Christianity in a manner commensurate with the themes of righteousness and justice, which they find in the pages of Scripture. But an imbalance has taken place, a loss of perspective that requires redressing if the full integrity and richness of the Christian experience is to be retrieved and revitalized in our day.

The argument of this project can be outlined in the following manner:

1. Western Christianity for nearly two centuries has adopted the priorities and techniques of the historical-critical method of literary interpretation. Much that can be commended has resulted, but it has also resulted in a reductionistic focus on the literal dimension to the loss of the spiritual, especially, as argued here, the anagogical. In many circles a kind of embarrassment of the anagogical has set in, further reducing its influence in the preaching and teaching of the Church.

2. Coterminous with these developments has been an increasing identification of Christian spirituality with morality.

Again, this development itself redressed previous omissions of faith and practice, but a model of moral imitation and a loss of the sense of mystical participation results when the ethical-imitative dimension is prioritized above all else. Fearful of being found "too heavenly minded to be of any earthly good," the Church today over-compensates and loses sight that only the heavenly minded are of any earthly good.

3. Resources for redressing these imbalances and reductions exists in Scripture itself and in the interpretive perspective and doctrines of the first eight centuries of the Church, commonly referred to as the patristic era. It is these resources and those contemporary thinkers influenced by them that this volume seeks to bring to bear in the present moment. The Church is at its strongest, the Christian experience is at its deepest, the world is most transformed when the body of Christ embraces its ascended identity in its Savior,and when individual members of Christ's body consent to the full riches of their inheritance in the Lord.

Anagogical interpretation of Scripture seeks to identify, highlight, and appropriate the ways in which Scripture points toward and instantiates the Church's participation in its heavenly existence. Anagogical interpretation highlights the eschatological tension between the "now" and "not yet" of the experience of redemption, but gives this tension an unapologetic priority over the way it is too often relegated to the backroom of "last things." In the anagogical perspective, the "last things" determines present experience now, even as full consummation awaits. We begin with the End in mind.

Some might associate the manner in which anagogy is being here described with the category of apocalypticism. They are indeed related, and the apocalyptic dimension of Scripture is a real and important element in biblical religion. However, the anagogical and apocalyptic are different.

Anagogy focuses on the union of the Church with Christ, and how each member of this body participates in and is assimilated into the full stature, the entire implications, of the cosmic redemption effective by the Father through his Son in the Holy Spirit.

The apocalyptic, on the other hand, focuses on the persecution and vindication of God's people. Apocalypticism reveals God's presence in the midst of his seeming absence on the battlefield of earth. Apocalypticism discloses who's on the inside and who's on the outside of God's redemptive purposes. Apocalypticism is therefore intentionally separative, and necessarily so. The persecuted people of God need to know that despite all appearances, God is present with them, he is in control of events, and he is on their side. All that opposes them and deceives the world is judged and will be defeated.

The apocalyptic element of Scripture is necessary for the Church in the militant dimension of its identity. The anagogical is necessary for its mystical dimension, and it is this dimension that the present project focuses upon.

The anagogical is, as already mentioned, related to the eschatological. Eschatology is the study of last things, which includes the heavenly and eternal in Christian theology. In its broadest sense, eschatology is a theology of time, of God's purposes within time, and of the direction in which God's purposes are moving. Christians are intimately caught-up in this time-bound trajectory of divine purposefulness. Anagogy illuminates these subject matters. The relationship between anagogy and eschatology is explored within this book

While addressed to all Christians as well as the academic community, this work does reflect the convictions and orientation of a Roman Catholic author. Therefore, for example, the word "church" will be frequently capitalized, indicative of the importance and priority ascribed to the Church by one committed to its *magisterium* or teaching authority. I seek to speak as a son of the Church, bringing forth "what is new and what is old" from her treasury of teachings and resources and deeply appreciative of the fresh sense of permission granted in the work of the Second Vatican Counsel for lay Catholics to read the Bible and make its worldview their own.

Among those aforementioned treasures of the Church is, for me personally, the work and witness of Joseph Ratzinger, Pope Benedict XVI. In his justly celebrated three-volume project *Jesus of Nazareth*, Pope Benedict summarized for a contemporary audience the basic way the Church has always sought to *exegete* ("bring out the meaning of") the Bible:

> I am convinced that good exegesis involves two stages. Firstly one has to ask what the respective authors intended to convey through their text in their own day—the historical component of exegesis. But it is not sufficient to leave the text in the past and thus relegate it to history. The second question posed by good exegesis must be: Is what I read here true? Does it concern me? If so, how?[3]

The anagogical sense of Scripture in its upward-leading, vision-transforming dynamic, is a vital aspect of answering that "how" of Pope Benedict's outline.

---

3. Pope Benedict XVI, *Jesus of Nazareth: The Infancy Narratives*, xi.

Acknowledgments

MUCH OF THE CONTENT in chapters 1–5 are derived from materials coauthored with Fr. Philip Krill. Previous work of his in relation to anagogy and spirituality deeply informs this book, as well as discussions he and I have had over the past three years. Since my reception into the Roman Catholic Church in 2017, no one has so encouraged me in my newfound Christian home than Fr. Phil. He has been particularly instrumental in pointing me toward a more consistently patristic vision of the gospel and of a more optimistic apprehension of our life and future in union with Christ. Few people that I know are so grounded in the conviction, with all its implications, of the Johannine proclamation that Jesus is "the expiation of our sins, and not for ours only but for the sins of the *whole world*" (1 John 2:2). This volume would simply not have come about without the initiative, research, and insights that he provides. This book is dedicated to him.

I want to acknowledge and thank Robin Parry and Matthew Wimer at Wipf and Stock for their invaluable editorial assistance.

Barbara Charalambidis once again performed the role of guardian of the electronic version of this project in its many permutations. Her friendship is a precious part of my life.

And finally, I wish to acknowledge my wife, Kathryn Edwina, a gift of God from the green valleys of Wales, and our children Lydia, Patrick, Peter, and Loryn.

Introduction

"GOD BECAME MAN SO man could become God."[1] This patristic axiom, known as the doctrine of deification or *theosis*, is a central, if often overlooked, mystery of the Christian faith. The classic, although certainly not sole passage from Scripture from which this doctrine emerges, is 2 Peter 1:4, ". . . that you may escape from the corruption that is in the world because of passion, and *become partakers of the divine nature.*"

The Christian experience is intended to be one of total transformation. The icon of the transfiguration depicts not only Christ's divinity but also the divinizing power of the Spirit at work in those united to him by faith and Baptism. Though addressing man at the level of his person, it is not an individualistic, private affair. In the incarnation, passion, resurrection, and ascension of God's only-begotten Son, all of humanity, indeed in some way all of the created cosmos, can be understood as being taken up into the life of God. The unfolding of the Christian mystery in time is the on-going fulfillment of Jesus' promise that "when I am lifted up, I will draw all men [or: 'all things'] to myself" (John 12:32).

The Church, the body of Christ, is therefore more than a voluntary association of people committed to a similar set of beliefs.

1. Athanasius, *On the Incarnation*, 54.

1

It is a *mystical body*, a *spiritual corporation*, united spiritually and sacramentally to a Head and sharing in all the redemptive and transformative—indeed deifying—benefits of his salvific achievement as well as his present ministry and reign over the world. The Church enjoys an ascended existence already by virtue of her union with Christ, even as it remains in an earthly and often suffering experience. The Christian life is one of faith by which the vicissitudes of present life are seen through the lens of revealed truths.

But to fully appreciate and appropriate the realities of this truth, it is necessary to develop an *anagogical imagination*,[2] and doing so involves an understanding of the gospel, as one popular author has put it, "with the End in mind."[3] *Anagogy* is about that end. *Anagogy* refers to spiritual realities understood as our "life in the risen Christ." Life "in Christ," as Saint Paul so frequently puts it, concerns the Christian's life united to Christ by personal faith and sacramental initiation. Such union with Christ transfers the Christian from a fundamental identity with Adam, the head of the human race, to a fundamental identity with Christ, the Son of God and Head of the Church. To be "in Christ" is to share in all that is true of Christ: a divine quality of life, sonship, righteousness, Spirit-empowerment, open and constant access to the Father in prayer. It is a life "hidden" from the world's comprehension and awaiting future vindication, a life that is ascended now and yet waiting for its public manifestation at the end of time.

In this sense, two biblical passages are key to a Christian's self-understanding:

> If then you have been raised with Christ, seek the things
> that are above, where Christ is, seated at the right hand
> of God. Set your minds on things that are above, not on
> things that are on earth. For you have died, and your
> life is hid with Christ in God. When Christ who is our

2. James Alison's work, with its many variations on the theme of developing "an eschatological imagination," suggests what is referred to here as an "anagogical imagination." See his *Raising Abel: The Recovery of the Eschatological Imagination*. The titles of this and Alison's book recall to mind the celebrated volume by David Tracy, *The Analogical Imagination* (1981).

3. Habit #2 in Covey, *Seven Habits of Highly Effective People*.

life appears, then you also will appear with him in glory.
(Col 3:1–4)

See what love the Father has given us, that we should
be called children of God; and so we are. The reason
why the world does not know us is that it did not know
him. Beloved, we are God's children now; it does not yet
appear what we shall be, but we know that when he appears we shall be like him, for we shall see him as he is.
And every one who thus hopes in him purifies himself
as he is pure. (1 John 3:1–3)

Anagogy, then, refers us to our *incorporation into* Christ, an
incorporation that is both *now* and *not yet* in it's full manifestation.
This "participation *in Christ*" is an anagogical movement; ours is
an existence of ascension, of being "lifted up" with and in Christ
and already seated with him at the right hand of the Father, as
Saint Paul so eloquently expresses it:

But God, who is rich in mercy, out of the great love with
which he loved us, even when we were dead through
our trespasses, made us alive together with Christ (by
grace you have been saved), and raised us up with him,
and made us sit with him in the heavenly places in
Christ Jesus, that in the coming ages he might show the
immeasurable riches of his grace in kindness toward us
in Christ Jesus. (Eph 2:4–7)

No dimension of Jesus' story is more foreign to modern sen-
sibilities than that of this ascension. "It seems too closely bound up
with a mythical vision of the world that we have long since been
unable to share."[4] But the mystery of Christ's ascension has nothing
to do with travel to outer space. On the contrary, "it is the 'space
travel' of the heart, from the dimension of self-enclosed isolation
to the new dimension of world-embracing love."[5] "'Ascension' does
not mean departure into a remote region of the cosmos but, rather,
the continuing closeness that the disciples experience so strongly

4. Benedict XVI, *Dogma and Preaching*, 311.
5. Benedict XVI, *Jesus of Nazareth: Holy Week*, 286.

3

that it becomes a source of lasting joy."[6] The ascension of Christ is the *apex* of the Jesus story, on which all other dimensions of Jesus' earthly life depend. It is also the crowning mystery to which the other events of his Paschal mystery point. Jesus has come from the Father, and he goes back to the Father (John 13:3). His departure from heaven and his return to his Father is the narrative framework in which are embedded the most profound mystical truths regarding the Word-made-flesh. The ascension of Jesus is the culmination of the incarnational mystery, revealing to those who have "eyes to see" and "ears to hear" (e.g., Matt 13:16) that the entirety of creation "now has a place in God."[7]

This book aims at reclaiming the anagogical imagination in order to share in God's own contemplation of the world—to better enable Christians in allowing their imaginations to be "lifted up" into his own and participate in his love and desire for all he has created. One author has called this process "acquiring an 'epistemic participation' in the Mind of Christ."[8] Saint Paul himself exhorts his audience to "have this mind among yourselves, which was in Christ Jesus" (Phil 2:5).

Projects such as this ride on the backs of underlying conversations and conflicts between different parties and movements of thought and practice. The first such conversation is about the contrast between the active and the contemplative as primary modes of Christian spirituality. This project affirms the legitimacy of both, but certainly places its thumb strongly on the contemplative side of the scale as a redress the overly activist emphasis found in much of American Christianity. While this is a project of primarily contemplative religion, it is not addressed to the monastic calling or to a Benedict Option approach to social life, valid as these are. It is addressed to members of the academy as well as interested laypeople who wish to consider the insights of two men, both with pastoral experience, both of a scholarly bent of mind, who desire to present

6. Benedict XVI, *Jesus of Nazareth: Holy Week*, 281.
7. Benedict XVI, *Dogma and Preaching*, 313.
8. Barron, *Priority of Christ*, esp. 153–71.

material and thoughts toward a renewal of Church life as the mid-point of the twenty-first-century approaches.[9]

Secondly, this volume brings together the distinctions and differences between Western and Eastern forms of Christianity. Both it and its authors are solidly in the Western Church, but the project draws strongly upon and is deeply influenced by the contributions of the Eastern "lung" of the Church. This is a not-too-subtle advocacy for the benefits that accrue when the insights of Eastern, Platonically inflected theology and practices are brought to bear in Catholic life.[10] Close to the center of this book, for example, is the doctrine of *deification*, something that is acknowledged in both Western and Eastern Churches but certainly finds greater emphasis in the East. This distinction in turn reflects differences in emphases and practices related to the understanding of salvation between the two wings or "lungs" of the Church.[11]

Third is a conversation between what can be called the neo-scholastic and the *ressourcement* schools of Catholic theology. This refers to movements of Catholic theological renewal and clarification that emerged in the early and mid-twentieth century. They are certainly not the only such movements, but both represent two major movements within Roman Catholicism that took matters of tradition and a desire to maintain a vibrant orthodoxy with great earnestness. The perceptive reader will find that this project follows a distinctly *ressourcement* approach to theology.

This work is, finally, an engagement with Scripture. While it is not an extended study of biblical hermeneutics *per se*, several terms and concepts must first be explained and considered in order to proceed meaningfully.

To even speak of an anagogical imagination in relation to Christian spirituality is to echo and draw upon an aspect of

9. The contribution of Fr. Philip Krill is acknowledged throughout this project.

10. For a study of the Platonic influence in Christian thought, see Louth, *Origins of the Christian Mystical Tradition*.

11. Pope Saint John Paul II used the analogy of "two lungs" to describe the Western and Eastern Churches in the encyclical *Ut Unum Sint* (1995).

biblical interpretation known as the anagogical sense of Scripture. The anagogical sense is part of a long tradition of Christian biblical interpretation that, since Saint Paul, has understood the Bible to be comprised of both "letter" and "spirit" (2 Cor 3:6). From this descends a long history of hermeneutics (or method of interpretation) that sought the meaning of God's word in what we today call its historical-critical sense and in its spiritual sense. Responsible Christian exegesis has always recognized and honored the fact that the Bible is made up of human words reflecting a human history and the cultures in which they were written. Catholic exegesis continues in this vein.[12]

At the same time, most Christian exegetes in the past were bishops and clergy concerned to communicate the applicable meaning of the words of Holy Writ to those in their care. Their concerns centered on inquiries such as, "What do these words (especially those of the Old Testament) have to do with us in our Christian context and in light of our allegiance to Jesus?" This is the "spiritual" dimension of Scripture in its first sense. In the earliest days of the Church, this "spiritual sense" focused on the apprehension of the presence of Christ in the Old Testament. To read the Old Testament in the Church by the Spirit was to increasingly perceive Jesus as the One in whom the Scriptures are completed and fulfilled.

To that end, a number of interpretive moves and techniques were deployed, some of which are found in the text of the New Testament itself. Saints Matthew and Paul, for example, employ aspects of rabbinic *midrash* in their use of Old Testament texts. Midrash involves an approach to the text of Scripture that seeks to find fresh

---

12. It needs to be emphasized that the historical-literal sense is of spiritual significance because the Judeo-Christian religion is grounded in the basic conviction that God has and continues to act and manifest himself on the stage of real human history. Matter matters and human history is significant because God addresses himself to his people in these realities. This distinguishes biblical religion from alternatives in which liberation is located in a repudiation of matter and time. For this and much of the subject matter of this chapter, see the Pontifical Biblical Commission, *Interpretation of the Bible in the Church.*

meaning in contexts beyond the text's originating framework.[13] Matthew's genealogy of Jesus, for example, reflects a midrashic adaptation of a complicated pedigree in order to illustrate the descent of Jesus from Abraham through David in such a way that the very structure of the genealogy forms a coded message for the discerning reader—that of the name of David.

Saint Paul of course finds what he calls an "allegory" in the stories of Sarah and Hagar in his Epistle to the Galatians. Allegory has a long story of origin stretching back to Hellenistic readings of Homer and the mythologies. Allegory as a method of textual interpretation aims to contemporize ancient texts in such ways that relevant morals or insights can be perceived afresh and applied in life. For Paul, the account of Sarah and Hagar becomes a portrait of two different lines of descent and legitimacy, pointing to the new covenant in Jesus. In the subsequent history of Christian biblical interpretation, allegory unfortunately comes to suffer from association with sometimes highly fanciful elaborations that seem to beg too many questions and take the texts far afield from anything related to their original intentions.

Another very important literary technique related to allegory but less inclined to excessive elaboration is that of *typology*. Again, Saint Paul provides a model: for example, drawing on the Old Testament accounts of the Red Sea and God's provision for Israel in the wilderness in 1 Corinthians 10:1-5, Paul identifies the Red Sea crossing with Baptism and the rock out of which saving water came with Christ. This is typology, the identification of "types" with their corresponding "antitypes," by which the gospel is found to be anticipated and validated in the only Bible the apostolic Church had access to, the Old Testament.

The Church subsequently elaborated on the "spiritual" sense of Scripture into a division of three types: the allegorical, the tropological (or moral), and the anagogical. It must be remembered that in early (or patristic) exegesis these divisions and differentiations were not so distinctly categorized. To read the Scriptures "spiritually" was to maintain the integrity of its originating

---

13. Bray, *Biblical Interpretation*, 56–69.

intentions (its "literal" sense) while at the same time plumbing the depths of its full salvific scope.[14]

An example of the sort of "spiritual" reading of biblical texts characteristic of the Fathers is found in seventh-century master Saint Maximus the Confessor. In his *Four Hundred Chapters on Love*, this seventh-century monastic theologian reflects on the implications of Psalm 23:

> "You have prepared a table for me, etc." *Table* here signifies practical virtue, for this was prepared by Christ "against those who afflict us." The *oil* which anoints the mind is the contemplation of creatures, the *cup* of God is the knowledge of God itself; his *mercy* is his Word and God. For through his incarnation he pursues us *all days* until he gets hold of those who are to be saved, as he did with Paul. The *house* is the kingdom in which all the saints will be restored. The *length of days* means eternal life.[15]

The anagogical sense of Scripture emerges from this desire to explore the depths of the spirituality of the Bible. "Let us expand the extent of the mystery still higher. Let us pursue the peaks of spiritual understanding." With two citations, by Origen and Saint Jerome respectively, Henri de Lubac opens the chapter on Anagogy and Eschatology in his multi-volume *Medieval Exegesis*. De Lubac reviews the tortuous etymology of the word *anagōgē* and concludes:

> The translator takes this word in the meaning that had become normal in the first centuries of our era and that the Neoplatonic school would settle upon: i.e. not in the sense of a "trip" or "passing through" as it had among the ancient Pythagoreans, but in the sense of a "climb" or an "ascent." The etymology bruited about would be explained by its equivalent "sursumductio"; it comes, as they say, from *ana*, which is "sursum" (upward) and *agōgē*, which is "ductio" (leading).[16]

---

14. Lubac, *Medieval Exegesis*, 1:66–74.

15. Maximus the Confessor, *Selected Writings*, 61.

16. Lubac, *Medieval Exegesis*, 2:179.

Again, this project, drawing on the tradition of different "senses" inherent in Scripture, seeks to reclaim the anagogical imagination, so active in earlier times, for our own day now. But some further terminology deserves prefatory attention.

"Sense" and "imagination" introduces to biblical hermeneutics terms associated with aesthetics. *Aesthesis*, the Greek term from which aesthetics is derived, means that which is related to sense perception. We have access to the world around us by means of our sense organs. In a secondary way the concept of sense is related to the perceived meaning of something. Something makes "sense" when we understand it. Sense then refers to the logic, the orientation, the trajectory of something, which gives it its intelligibility. Sense in both its primary and secondary meanings assumes a capacity to meaningfully encounter and access the object in consideration. This capacity can be called a *sensibility*, again a term redolent with aesthetic significance. Sensibility refers to a condition in which one can pick up the cues and clues, the subtleties and insinuations, of a given encounter or study. Developing such an effective sensibility towards something, however, takes time and practice. One has to indwell the world through a painting or a piece of music or a work of literature or a scientific methodology in order to develop a sensibility to its unique mode of perception. Immersion in Scripture and its world is likewise a requirement if one is to develop a sensibility with regard to the multivalent nature of the Bible.

Finally, this work speaks of a form of *imagination*. The root of imagination of course is "image," and the imagination first of all is the capacity to engage with imagery. Some people are naturally gifted in this, while for others it is a struggle, but for all it requires time and a receptivity for such imagination to develop.[17] An anagogical imagination, for example, is one that can begin to think *proleptically* about the Christian life, that is to see in the minds eye one's fellowship and inclusion in a future mode of existence manifest in the present. To this end, icons can become an effective resource for religious formation. This

17. For further reflections on these matters, see McCullough, *Sense and Spirituality*, 45–57.

9

project commends in particular iconographic presentations of the transfiguration of the Lord. Here we encounter the divine in human flesh, and human flesh infused with divinizing grace. This is the anagogical destiny of those united to the Lord. That incident, which occurred "there and then" in salvation history has significance for Christians in their lives "here and now." Bridging this "hermeneutical gap," as its often called, is what developing an anagogical imagination is all about.

The Second Vatican Counsel (1962–65) released immense amounts of new and creative energies in the Catholic Church. Among them was a renewed sense of permission for the laity to engage with Scripture. This has revolutionized the depth of knowledge of the faith among the laity and promises to continue to do so in the future. What remains to accomplish now is the retrieval of a participatory relationship with God's purposes in creation and redemption, a kind of spirituality that some would call *mystical*. But this is a mystical spirituality that not only situates one's personal life within a new horizon, as salubrious as this is, but sees God's redemptive purposes now taking on cosmic dimensions as well.

Too often Catholics, and indeed Christians of all stripes, experience what can be called a reductionistic faith. In an American context, that involves what sociologist Christian Smith calls "moralistic, therapeutic deism."[18] God is perceived as someone "up there" who is only concerned with good behavior and appropriate affect. One somehow connects with the deity on the basis of one's best efforts, and ministry is evaluated on its delivery of goods in the most accessible and convenient manner. Critical of similar patterns in Catholic Christianity, Pope Benedict XVI referred to the French-coined phrase *maladie catholique:* "a special neurosis that is the product of a warped pedagogy so exclusively concentrated on the Fourth and Sixth Commandments that the resultant complex with regard to authority and purity renders the individual incapable of free self-development."[19]

18. Smith, *Soul Searching*, 162.
19. Ratzinger, *Principles of Catholic Theology*, 77.

The anagogical vision proposed in this volume is an antidote to these kinds of reductionism. Anagogy raises the pitch of the Christian experience by opening up an orientation toward Scripture and worship in which the light of the resurrection and ascension illumines and interprets every aspect of belief and praxis. Such was the vision that accounts for the theological appeal of two recent papacies, those of Pope Saint John Paul II and Benedict XVI. Most of all, it is the vision of the early Church Fathers, such as Irenaeus of Lyon and Ignatius of Antioch, Cyril of Alexandria and Cyril of Jerusalem, Origen and Athanasius, Saints Macrina and Monica, Gregory of Nyssa and Maximus the Confessor. These, many from the Eastern half of the Church, are hardly household names in much of the Catholic world, but are sources to which this project primarily turns.[20]

The first and great antidote to the kind of functional unitarianism or deism suggested above is the doctrine of the Trinity. This revelation of God not only grounds the radically personalistic quality of God's very existence, but grounds all consideration of human incorporation into it. The key is Jesus, who is able to share in our humanity and communicate his divinity to us. It is because of the Son of God's capacity to lift his people up into himself that talk about an "anagogical imagination" is even possible. Drawing on the implications of the Counsel of Chalcedon, Jesus is understood as the one who is both divine and human "without confusion or change" and is therefore able to unite his people into his divinity without diminishing their humanity; assimilation without annihilation is possible in the logic of Chalcedon. This is the metaphysical grounding of all Christian anagogy or mystical spirituality and is the grounding for the retrieval of the kind of depth our ephemeral and thin society resists and retreats from.

---

20. The names of these Eastern Fathers are found throughout the *Catechism of the Catholic Church*, no more so than in the fourth and final section addressing Christian prayer. The primary author of this section was Fr. Jean Corbon, a priest of the Byzantine Rite Melkite Church. This section of the Catechism is a wonderful resource for informing an anagogical imagination, and Fr. Corbon, *Wellspring of Worship*, is highly recommended as well.

The new Pentecost, so greatly desired by Saint Pope John XXIII, who initiated Vatican II, depends for its permanent manifestation on a revival of the Catholic faith that begins and ends with the mystery of the Trinity. "If then you have been raised with Christ, seek the things that are above," Saint Paul exhorts, and "set your minds on things that are above, not on things that are on earth." An anagogical, Trinitarian orientation is the only foundation for a vision of incorporation into the divine life through the sacramental mysteries of the Church.[21]

If the language of an "anagogical imagination" sounds strange, it is because contemporary sacramental and ecclesial vision needs a kind of expansion as well as a deepening. To this end, the Church must learn to breathe with both lungs, as John Paul II was fond of saying. By this he meant with both the Eastern and Western Catholic traditions of mystical and contemplative reflection on the mysteries of the faith. Benedict XVI too beckoned toward a more profound, personal, and contemplative approach to these matters: "Christianity is not an intellectual system, a collection of dogmas, or a moralism. Christianity is instead an encounter, a love story; it is an event."[22]

This book follows in a general way the outline of the *Catechism of the Catholic Church*, addressing itself to matters of creed (dogma), cult (liturgy), code (ethics), and contemplation (Christian prayer), with a focus on the anagogical mysteries of Jesus' resurrection and ascension:

> The Symbol of the faith confesses the greatness of God's gifts to man in his work of creation, and even more in redemption and sanctification. What faith confesses, the sacraments communicate: by the sacraments of rebirth, Christians have become "children of God," "partakers of the divine nature." Coming to see in the faith their new dignity, Christians are called to lead henceforth a life "worthy of the gospel of Christ." They are made capable

21. Much of the introductory material here is further explored in Krill and McCullough, *Life in the Trinity*.

22. Benedict XVI, "Homily for Msgr. Luigi Giusanni," 685. See also Benedict XVI, *Deus Caritas Est*, §1.

of doing so by the grace of Christ and the gifts of his Spirit, which they receive through the sacraments and through prayer.[23]

"God became man so man could become God." In his incarnation, Jesus assumes all things into himself. In his resurrection and ascension, he "lifts up" a redeemed and re-created world to his Father. Christian faith comes alive when the faithful are able to understand and experience their lives as incorporated into the life of the Trinity through their participation in Jesus' divine-human person and purposes.

This book is grounded theologically on a twin-paradox: in his incarnation, Jesus never left heaven, and in his resurrection and ascension, Jesus never left the earth.[24] Mysteriously, Christ has incorporated both heaven and earth into his ever-living, ever-active, filial relationship of self-surrendering love with his Father. It is assimilation into this Trinitarian mystery, through participation in Jesus' prayer to his Father, that constitutes the core identity of members of this mystical body, the Church. The aim of this book is to furnish the reader with the beginnings of such an imagination.

---

23. CCC 1692.

24. A frequent theme in the writings of Benedict XVI, e.g., *Dogma and Preaching*.

I

God Descending

*The Doctrine of the Trinity in Relation
to Anagogy*

Aristotelian philosophy, as we well know, tells us that between God and man there is only a non-reciprocal relationship. Man refers to God, but God, the Eternal, is in Himself, He does not change; He cannot have this relationship today and another relationship tomorrow. He is within Himself, He does not have *ad extra* relations. It is a very logical term, but it is also a word that makes us despair: so God Himself has no relationship with me. With the Incarnation, with the event of the *Theotokos*, this radically changed, because God drew us into Himself and God Himself is the relationship and allows us to participate in His interior relationship. Thus we are in His being Father, Son and Holy Spirit, we are within His being in relationship, we are in relationship with Him and He truly created a relationship with us. At that moment, God wished to be born from woman and to remain Himself always: this is the great event.[1]

---

1. "Meditation of His Holiness Benedict XVI during the First General Congregation Special Assembly for the Middle East Synod of Bishops, Synod Hall, Monday, 11 October, 2010," cited in Schumacher, *Trinitarian Anthropology*, 25.

EVERYTHING BEGINS AND ENDS with our conception of God. Pope Benedict XVI (Joseph Ratzinger), in the epigraph above, articulates the outline and logic of the Christian doctrine of the Trinity in contrast to mere monotheism. The one God's very existence—prior to anything else—is *intrinsically relational*, and so the capacity for relationship, and the incorporation of others into that relationship, is entirely possible and logically coherent.

Many Catholics, however, live with a generic, impersonal, "Aristotelian" idea of God. Theirs is a liturgical Trinitarianism but a functional unitarianism. "God" is an amorphous, homogeneous concept, sometimes referring to a person, sometimes to a power, sometimes to an object, separated and above and beyond the world he created. They do not deny the existence of the Trinity or the Church's teaching in this regard; they are simply *experientially* ignorant of it. Benedict XVI impugns such a view of God as "non-trinitarian monotheism."[2]

Part of the problem is one of a tradition of language used in reference to God. From the pre-Socratics through the neo-scholastics of the present time, Western metaphysics and theology have developed a rich tradition of perceiving God as Pure Act (*Ipsum esse subsistens*—"the sheer act of to-be itself") in an attempt to understand and articulate the mystery of the Divine. In particular, Saint Thomas Aquinas' revolutionary way of grasping the coinherent yet utterly independent relation of the Creator and creation continues to inform and inspire reflection on the mystery of God's immanent and transcendent connection to the cosmos.

Despite Saint Thomas' humble admission that "Since we are not able to know what God is, only what God is not, we are not able to consider in regard to how God is, but rather how he is not,"[3] we today must extend our search for the "unknowable" God who is "beyond being," the "God without being," at least as defined in reified, metaphysical terms. This necessity leads beyond even the apophatic tradition of Pseudo-Dionysius and his successors. It leads towards the way of anagogy, based on the implications of the

2. Ratzinger, *Feast of Faith*, 21.
3. Aquinas, *Summa Theologia* I.3 Prologue.

Trinitarian conception of God where divine personhood precedes being, and where the Trinitarian communion of persons (*communio personarum*) provides the Source (*Arche*), Goal (*Telos*), and Intelligibility (*Logos*) of all created forms and relationships.

It is the early Church Fathers of the first eight centuries of the Christian era, familiar as they were with all forms of classical philosophy, who provide a perspective that presupposes and perfects whatever wisdom philosophy can provide. The early Church encountered the God of Israel in his Son, Jesus, who had now given his Spirit to this community which he had founded. Though still developing the technical language by which they would express this experience, the Church was thoroughly Trinitarian in all its activities and beliefs. Likewise, the Church was animated by an eschatological vision in which the End is in the Beginning, the future creates and reveals the meaning of the past, and a glorious trans-temporal *pleroma*, a "fullness," is the purpose for which the temporal process exists. The primary biblical source for this is Saint Paul, who speaks expansively of the Church as "[Christ's] body, the fullness of him who fills all in all" (Eph 1:23). Licensed by such language, the Fathers, especially the Cappadocians (Basil the Great, his brother Gregory of Nyssa, and their associate Gregory of Nazianzus), taught that eschatology precedes and unveils the purposes of protology. For them, *God began with the end in mind.* Just as Michelangelo saw a finished, exquisitely beautiful statue of David when others saw only a block of marble, God envisioned a perfected cosmos with the whole of humanity functioning as one with its eternal High Priest when he said, "Let there be light" as the first act making possible this glorious *pleroma.*

How, then, did the early Church connect these truths about God with Christian experience and self-understanding? There is no simple or easy way to explain what transpired, and transpires, in the greatest minds and hearts of the saints of the Christian Church. But in all the conceptual complexity a brilliance shines forth, especially in the *mystagogical catecheses* of the early Church. Following this patristic tradition, we seek to re-acquire the anagogical sense of what is communicated to us, both in Scripture and in the liturgical life of the Church. Only so can we properly approach and begin to understand the Trinitarian and eschatological orientation of Christian existence.

Theological reflection in the early Church was driven by participation in what the Fathers simply called "the mysteries," that is, the liturgical celebrations of Baptism and Holy Eucharist. As a divine person, Jesus assumed a human nature to achieve our redemption and provide for our deification, and now "All that was visible in our Savior has passed over into his mysteries."[4] The Holy Spirit effects our divinization "in Christ," to use the familiar Pauline phrase, through our participation in the liturgical life of his Church. As Popes John Paul II and Benedict XVI have said repeatedly, *the Eucharist makes the Church and the Church celebrates the Eucharist.*[5] A person is mystically engrafted into the living person of Jesus in the primordial mystery of Baptism. This union of Vine to branches (John 15:1–5) is strengthened in Confirmation and consummated in Holy Communion. Everything about the Christian faith, starting with God himself, is a *relationship of communion.* The mystery of the divine *communio* of the Trinity is the defining archetype of the Christian existence. Apart from Baptism, Chrismation, and Holy Eucharist, there is no true, substantial communion with Jesus Christ, through whom the faithful are ingrafted into the divine *communio.* Yes, saving faith "comes through hearing" (Rom 10:17; Gal 3:2), but the encounter with the gospel issues ineluctably into the imperative to "be baptized!" (Acts 2:38; 10:48). Even Saint Paul, immediately after his encounter with the risen Christ on the road to Damascus, "was baptized" and thereafter regained his sight (Acts 9:18). Baptism effects incorporation; the Eucharist effects divinization. This is the manner by which patristic theology articulates the Christian life.

It was because the early Church experienced a saving union with Christ in its sacramental mysteries that its greatest saints were

---

4. Pope Saint Leo the Great, *Sermon 74*, cited in CCC 1115.

5. A theme in part derived from and emphasized in the work of Henri de Lubac, a great representative of the *ressourcement* movement.

impelled and enabled to reflect on the risen Christ revealed and made present in these self-same mysteries. Working backwards from their encounter with Father, Son, and Holy Spirit in the sacraments of Baptism and Holy Eucharist, the Church Fathers discerned how Christ came to "lift them up" into participation in his own Trinitarian life. They found anticipations of this, of course, in the Scriptures. The Jewish people had known God as intensely personal, even intimate with them. On Mount Sinai and elsewhere, he even "visited his people" in their need. He condescended to meet them in sacred and specially consecrated places. But the possibility that the almighty YHWH could ever "become man" was "unthinkable, impossible, unimaginable!"[6] As radical as God's loving self-limitation may have been at times for his chosen people, "it had to stop short of one final logical development . . . that of the Son, who gives himself and lets himself be given, and that of the Spirit, who lets himself be 'poured out' and sent."[7] Only the Church, the *corpus mysticum* of the Messiah comprised of both Jews and gentiles, was in a position to discern that the very one who had bequeathed his disciples the mysteries of the "living water" (Baptism) and the "bread of eternal life" (Eucharist) was himself the way to the Father and the sender of the Holy Spirit.

Within this perception, liturgical prayer and worship likewise lie at the heart of life in Christ. These activities are the *theologia prima* of the Christian Church. Prayer, and the depth of our prayer, is the first and foremost measure of our relationship with God. *Lex orandi, lex credendi*: the law of praying [is] the law of believing. Christian prayer in this perspective is essentially a participation in the prayer of Jesus; Christians understand their address to the Father as "through Christ" and "in his name." Prayer and worship involves the assumption of the Church and all her members into the eternal self-surrender of the Son to the Father, effected through

---

6. To quote Tevye in *The Fiddler on the Roof*. One should be mindful, however, of the *theophanies* (divine manifestations) that occur throughout the Old Testament and how these were seen to prefigure and anticipate the miracle of the incarnation.

7. Schönborn, *God Sent His Son*, 116.

the sacraments.[8] These reflections are constitutive of an anagogical apprehension of Christian existence because they lift such reflection up and into an identification with Christ.

The development of Trinitarian theology and its many implications was a direct result of the Church's ongoing contemplation of the fontal mysteries at the heart of its liturgical life. As the proclamation of Jesus as Lord spread, the philosophical systems and naturalistic religions of the pagans were at once judged and redeemed by their encounter with the celebration of the Christian mysteries. The thinkers of the ancient world were challenged by the message of the incarnation and its implications for their religion and their lives. Whereas "God" for them had been an inscrutable, immutable, unchangeable, and altogether impassible monistic "ground of being," the advent of Jesus Christ revealed something entirely new. Like persons waking from a dream, they discovered a God whose primary *name is Father*, whose *face is Jesus*, and whose *presence is Holy Spirit*: a God whose name is his very being: "I am who am," God had said to Moses (Exod 3:14). So too with Jesus: "She will bear a son, and you shall call his name Jesus, for he will save his people from their sins" (Matt 1:21). Being and personhood were seen to be identical in the Trinitarian mystery. Personhood precedes being in God, and being *is* communion in God. "Existence" is a function of God's triune personhood, not vice versa. The Fathers of the early Church experienced God not as an abstract first cause or mysterious summation of being, but as a tri-hypostatic presence in whom all things find their *raison d'être*. For the early Church, Father, Son, and Holy Spirit are seen to establish, support, and sustain all manner and form of existence within and outside of the Trinitarian life.[9]

---

8. A recurring theme in the writings of Benedict XVI, e.g., "The Christian confession of faith comes from participating in the prayer of Jesus, from being drawn into his prayer and being privileged to behold it; it interprets the experience of Jesus' prayer, and its interpretation of Jesus is correct because it springs from a sharing in what is most personal and intimate to him." Ratzinger, *Behold the Pierced One*, 13.

9. Krill and McCullough, *Life in the Trinity*, 33–37.

The proposal advanced in this project involves a re-appropriation of these convictions fashioned to speak to the needs of today. Part of this is admittedly intellectual, involving a process of *ressourcement*, a "return to the sources," particularly those of the Greek-speaking Church, and a fresh appreciation of the dynamics of *mystagogy* and *anagogy*. It is also a deeply contemplative effort, driven by prayer, liturgy, and the *lectio divina* or "sacred reading." "Contemplation," Pope Benedict XVI wrote, "aims at creating within us a truly wise and discerning vision of reality as God sees it, and at forming within us 'the mind of Christ' (I Cor. 2:16)."[10] This is what some might refer to as *mystical spirituality*. It apprehends a vision of God's intentions for humanity referred to as *deification* that begins and ends with an immersion in the reality of the Trinity and a theology that prayerfully reflects upon him "according to the Scriptures," an exercise that the early church called knowing Christ according to the rule of faith.[11] Regardless of the terms and phrases we use, only a more contemplative, anagogical, and explicitly Trinitarian Catholicism that will renew the Church in the difficult days that still lie ahead.

---

10. Benedict XVI, *Verbum Domini*, 87.
11. A theme explored in O'Keefe and Reno, *Sanctified Vision*.

2

Scripture as Medium of Encounter

How, then, is Scripture to be read in light of these convictions? More to the point, how is the record of salvation history with Jesus as its keystone, with the Church as the already-ascended body of Christ, and with human incorporation into the life of God as guiding themes to be both understood and appropriated meaningfully? These are the questions that can be met with an anagogical imagination. Sources for this very kind of imagination and vision are found in the tradition of patristic exegesis.

An episode such as the fall of Adam and Eve can be taken as a case in point for how a tradition situates and explicates the significance of a biblical narrative. The view prevalent in Western Christendom, at least since the time of Saint Augustine, sees original sin as a violation of God's commandment, resulting in guilt, shame, expulsion from the state of grace, and subsequent punishment. This forensic model of the fall was never adopted by the Christian East. Instead, the sin of Adam and Eve was turning from their contemplative vision of God, preferring the creation to the Creator as the object of their desire. This resulted in a corruption of human nature requiring the healing salve of God's salvation. Both of these models of the fall have in common a linear, historical narrative according to which God brought creation into being, followed by Adam and Eve who used their God-given freedom "to break from their Creator, thus plunging the world into sin and mortality, a condition in which it languished while the work of salvation was gradually being prepared, culminating in the Incarnation of Christ."[1] The preoccupation of the Western Church however, "with monotonous regularity since Thomas Aquinas and Duns Scotus" involves asking of hypothetical questions such as "whether Christ would have become man even if there had been no Fall."[2] These lines of inquiry tend toward a retributive understanding of God's purposes and a primarily forensic conception of redemption which obscures a larger, more graceful picture of redemption.

Saint Irenaeus, for example, articulates an alternative approach toward the incarnation:

> Since he who saves already existed, it was necessary that
> he who would be saved should come into existence, that
> the One who saves should not exist in vain.[3]

In the Irenaean perspective, Jesus is the solution, so to speak, before there ever was a problem. Jesus is the Savior *prior to* anything or anyone needing to be saved. As Savior, he enables us to see the problem (the fall) for what it really is—the occasion for the Son of God to reveal himself. For salvation is the person of Jesus himself. His generation as Son in the "immanent Trinity" is revealed to us in his mission as Savior and Redeemer in the "economic Trinity." The identity of Jesus as Son and Savior precedes and defines, pre-exists and creates, the entire network and natural conditions of historical existence for which he was pre-ordained by his Father as its one and only Redeemer.

Insights such as these can revolutionize instinctual ways of imagining both history and biblical interpretation. If Jesus

1. Behr, *Mystery of Christ*, 77.

2. Behr, *Mystery of Christ*, 78.

3. Irenaeus, *Against Heresies*, III.22.3, in Richardson, *Early Christian Fathers*, 378–80.

is Redeemer already in the Trinity, then our world—both in its pristine and fallen condition—was created *in order for* the Son to gather it to himself in its fulfillment. The world's history must be seen first and foremost in this anagogical light. The world was created for Jesus to save, indeed to assume into himself, thus divinizing it. It was neither a surprise nor a shock to God for which he was forced, as it were, to concede a solution. Speculation about the fall, sin, guilt, and healing of humanity must not be allowed to obscure the more primordial mystery that Jesus is the pre-existent Savior in the grand narrative of things. In this perception, Jesus does *not* come into the world as its Redeemer *because of* the fall. The event of original sin, real though it is, is in a sense irrelevant to the coming of the Christ. The world was created as it is—in all its inherent contingency, potential imperfection, and susceptibility to sin and apostasy—precisely and exclusively in view of the identity of Jesus as Son and Savior in the bosom of his Father. The freedom of God bespeaks an initiative *fully independent* of the uses or misuses of human freedom on the part of the creatures. This underscores a relation with the world grounded totally in grace, not necessity. Like Jesus' identity as Savior, grace is intrinsic to God's relationship with man, not a concession or "Plan B" made in light of unexpected events.

This way of imaging Jesus' relationship to the world—a world that his Father created for his Son's good pleasure—can seem strange and counter-intuitive. This is because many contemporary Christians are far removed from the patristic vision that championed it. But it can open its recipients up towards a fuller appreciation for the implications of Saint Paul's writings, especially in documents such as the Epistles to Ephesians and Colossians, as well as a more optimistic, expectant way of imaging God's love and of its prevailing presence in all things in general. This is what anagogical contemplation on the scope of the gospel can accomplish.

Contemplatively encountering Jesus in the liturgy of the Church and according to the rule of faith (as formulated in the tradition and the creeds) can be seen in the way that the early Church discriminated between orthodoxy and heresy long before the full canon of Scripture was completed. None of the challenges to the Christian faith in the early centuries could be answered by an appeal to Scripture alone, since "what scripture is and how it is to be read are the very points at issue."[4] Nor can the "meaning" of Scripture be extricated by a rigorous reconstruction either of the historical events of the past or the etymological development of the words. The so-called "historical-critical" approach to the Bible has borne much fruit, but is ultimately as insufficient as is the Protestant notion of *sola scriptura* to furnish us with an understanding of what the Scripture really means. For the "meaning" of the Scripture in an ultimately anagogical perspective is *Jesus himself.* The interpretive key for the whole of the Bible, Old and New Testaments, is the same key for everything in the Christian life: Jesus himself in his crucified, resurrected, and ascended glory. Jesus is the one and only "meaning" of the Scriptures—this is the supreme anagogy. As Pope Benedict has said, "all Christian theology, if it is to be true to its origin, must be first and foremost a theology of Resurrection. It must be a theology of Resurrection before it is a theology of the sinner; it must be a theology of Resurrection before it is a theology of the metaphysical Sonship of God. It can be a theology of the Cross but only as and with the framework of Resurrection."[5] Further, the mystery of the resurrection, precisely as an eschatological event, "is the good tidings that the power of death, the one constant of history, has, in a single instance, been broken by the power of God and that history has thus been imbued with an entirely new hope. . . . [T]he core of the gospel consists in the good tidings of the Resurrection, and, consequently in the good tidings of God's action, which precedes all human doing."[6]

From an anagogical point of view, then, we extend Cardinal Ratzinger's eschatological insight about Jesus resurrection to include his ascension and "coming again in glory." As noted above the ascension in particular has experienced an eclipse in the mind and imaginations of Christians for many years. This neglect is

4. Behr, *Mystery of Christ*, 46.

5. Ratzinger, *Principles of Catholic Theology*, 184–85.

6. Ratzinger, *Principles of Catholic Theology*, 185.

wrapped up in a loss of appreciation of the significance of Christ's humanity and of our sacramental access to in the Eucharist. British theologian David Brown expresses regret for this eclipse and emphasizes the significance of the ascension:

> That this is in fact the situation is suggested by the way in which Ascension Day is now treated as a sort of minor appendix to Easter rather than its culmination, in the permanent exaltation of humanity into the life of God. For most of Christian history the Ascension was seen as mattering not simply because Christ could then be treated as forerunner of our own future destiny, but more importantly because only through incorporation into that humanity was it thought that our own salvation was possible. Through mingling with what was incorruptible our own corruption would eventually be transformed also into incorruptibility. The divine nature in Christ renders his body incorruptible and so through association with that body our own too could achieve a similar status.[7]

One can now gain a greater understanding the liturgical and sacramental implications of Jesus' ascended identity. It was not the crucifixion nor the empty tomb nor even the appearances of the risen Christ that were in themselves the starting point for Christianity as a faith, a religion. It was rather in the encounter with him "in the breaking of the bread" that their "eyes were opened" (Luke 24:31). Here, in the Emmaus Road episode, the union of word and sacrament completes and puts participants in contact with the Living Lord. Here he is revealed. Seeing Jesus according to the "rule of faith" and "according to the Scriptures" enables us to recognize him in the Eucharist. Conversely, knowing him as risen, exalted, and coming again in the mystery of the Eucharist allows us to discern him ever more present in every passage of the Bible.

A religious reading of Scripture—*lectio divina*—is meant to be an *event*, an *encounter*, not only an exercise or an investigation. This is why Scripture was originally read primarily in liturgical

---

7. Brown, *God and Grace of Body*, 408–9.

settings and why this remains the privileged place for its meaningful reception. This is something given great emphasis in the writings of Pope Benedict.[8] Hearing the Bible read in the context of "the breaking of the bread," is where eyes and ears are opened afresh to encounter the Risen Lord present among his people. Here the proclamation of the Scripture is an encounter with Jesus in his crucified and ascended glory. This encounter is made possible by the Holy Spirit, who always prepares, makes present, and brings us into intimate communion with the Risen Christ.

8. Benedict XVI, *Verbum Domini*, 52–55.

3

Tradition and Contemplation in Biblical Interpretation

IT IS IMPORTANT TO recall that in Catholic Christianity, Scripture and tradition form a seamless whole grounded in a common source—the gospel.[1] Scripture is a product of the Church (in terms of human authorship and canonization), yet the Bible continually refines and purifies the Church. Jesus is present in both word and sacrament, Scripture and tradition. He is the *Urgrund*—the primal source—who abides in and works through all the elements of the faith. One cannot return often enough to this transcendental truth of Jesus as the Source-Center of both Bible and Church. He is the abiding presence who gives coherence, meaning, and definition to all "holy things" that his Spirit communicates to his people.

Catholic biblical studies, especially since the late-nineteenth century, has affirmed that a real history of people and events are enshrined within the pages of Scripture. Texts such as that produced by the Pontifical Biblical Commission in 1993 provide a brief but masterful overview of the development of Catholic

---

1. CCC 80. One could include the Anglican Church, especially in its Anglo-Catholic wing, as well as the Orthodox Church, in this characterization.

biblical interpretation.[2] Since the pontificates of Leo XIII and Pius XII, Catholic scholarship has embraced the tools of historical and literary criticism, both in order to achieve an "objective" perception of the biblical text as well as to gain insights into how that text addresses and seeks to persuade its recipients with its life-changing message. The "literal sense" of Scripture since the nineteenth century has been the focus of what is referred to as the "historical-critical method." While approved and validated, like all methods it is fraught with potential pitfalls, not the least of which is a reduction of Scripture to simply questions of sources, editing, and what-happened-then-and-there. A "faith hermeneutic" respects and draws from the benefits of historical studies, but continues on in a deeply *confessional* perspective. Appropriating the full benefits of the scriptural word involves the "spiritual senses" of Scripture, of which the anagogical imagination is one such orientation.

From an anagogical perspective, Scripture is read and *indwelled* from above, as it were, not only from below.[3] We begin with the End in mind. This means reading the Scriptures is something quite different from the notion of "history" as used by modern historians. "Salvation history" involves seeing the events recorded in Scripture "in the light of Christ" and according to the rule of faith (which was eventually formalized in the Nicene Creed). It means seeing the resurrection and ascension of Jesus as indicative of his eternal identity and of our future destiny, a destiny so secure that it can—indeed must—shape our present faith and experience. An anagogical imagination is capable of *seeing all of history as a preparation by the Father and the Holy Spirit for the Son to exercise his merciful redemption and assimilate all things into his humanized divinity so that "God might be all in all"* (1 Cor 15:28).

Clearly this involves more than reconstructing a merely chronological account of things "as they really happened," as

---

2. Pontifical Biblical Commission, *Interpretation of the Bible in the Church*.

3. The concept of "indwelling" a problem or question is derived from the realm of epistemology and is especially associated with the work of Michael Polanyi. In terms of its religious significance, see Loder, *Logic of the Spirit*, 113; Edwards, *Creation's Beauty as Revelation*, 79–83; Sire, *Naming the Elephant*, 104–5.

significant as that is. The "quest for the historical Jesus," for example, seeks the meaning of Jesus in light of the cultural and
political context of that time and place. But as Pope Benedict
XVI reminds us:

> Scripture must be interpreted in the same Spirit in which
> it was written [maintaining] three fundamental criteria
> for an appreciation of the divine dimension of the Bible:
> 1) the text must be interpreted with attention to *the unity
> of the whole of Scripture*, 2) account is be taken of the *liv-
> ing Tradition of the whole Church*; and, finally, 3) respect
> must be shown for *the analogy of faith*. "Only where both
> methodological levels, the historical-critical and the
> theological, are respected, can one speak of a theological
> exegesis, an exegesis worthy of [the Bible.]"[4]

Pope Benedict was both a supporter and critic of the historical-critical method. While acknowledging its invaluable contributions to our understanding of the Bible, Benedict was deeply
aware and indeed wary of the ideological import of the method.
Benedict developed what he called "a critique of the critique"
that sifts the weeds from the wheat in post-patristic exegesis.[5] His
overall point about the so-called "historical-critical" method is
that at bottom it is more than a method. It is a value-laden theory
of interpretation. The findings of the historical-critical method
can be argued and debated on their own empirical merits. It is the
deeper ideological assumptions of the method that can turn this
investigatory method into a philosophically biased instrument
for the deconstruction of the Christian faith.

Inviting us to embrace a hermeneutic of faith that includes yet transcends the historical-critical method, Benedict

4. Benedict XVI, *Verbum Domini*, 34, quoting *Dei Verbum*, 107. The
phrase "analogy of faith" is used in Catholic hermeneutics. It refers to the aim
of maintaining a balance and relationship between a particular exegesis and
the larger body of Catholic doctrine and tradition. See Brian E. Daley, "Knowing God in History and in the Church: *Dei Verbum* and "*Nouvelle Théologie*,"
in Flynn and Murray, *Ressourcement*, 334.

5. For a treatment of Benedict's hermeneutics, see Hahn, *Covenant and
Communion*, esp. 24–45.

highlighted "the dynamism and infinite depth" of the living Word. Because Jesus is the "Word within the words" of Scripture, no historical or critical analysis can understand or perceive the intention, meaning, or intentional plenitude of the sacred text and its authors.[6] God speaks, and has spoken, in and through the words of Scripture. Scripture is a living Word, especially when proclaimed in the eucharistic assembly. When considering the purpose and interpretation of the Bible, Benedict counseled that we must believe that *God can enter history without ceasing to be himself.* This is what it means to regard the Liturgy of the Word as a *kerygmatic event.* In the Liturgy of the Word, it is Jesus himself who addresses us, calling us to conversion, healing us of our wounds, instilling salvific faith in our hearts.

As an alternative to a "hermeneutic of suspicion," often associated with sole reliance on various historical-critical methods, Benedict proposed a "hermeneutic of faith" and a "hermeneutic of continuity."[7] According to this approach, the key assumptions of the patristic theology about God and the Bible remain legitimate, relevant, and deserving of revival. At the same time, it acknowledges and incorporates what is best about the historical-critical method.

Employing Benedict's hermeneutic of faith and continuity, we can outline some guiding principles for a closer reading of the Bible. These principles include the following:

- That Scripture, while consisting of diverse genres and originating contexts, forms a unified whole, created and rendered coherent by the presence of a single divine author—the Holy Spirit.

- The rule of faith as ultimately expressed in the classic creeds of the Church, provides guardrails, as it were, for the proper reading and interpretation of Scripture.

6. A frequent theme in Benedict's magisterium; see *Verbum Domini,* 44.

7. For a description of Benedict's "hermeneutic of faith," see *Verbum Domini,* 31, 35, 39, 45, 47. See also, Benedict XVI, *Jesus of Nazareth: Holy Week,* xvii.

- That the Bible is authoritative, i.e., the measure and means of properly understanding all things human and ecclesial. This refers back to the elusive phrase of "the analogy of faith."

- That God's Word is living and creative. Scripture is an ongoing *encounter* (a favored and frequently used word in Benedict's writings) with the "God who speaks," requiring a contemplative attitude and an "ascesis of the heart" as conditions its for proper understanding.

- Familiarity with the typological codes in Scripture, how figures and events in the Old Testament anticipate figures and events in the New, and indeed how the entire New Testament is a wholesale anagogy of the Old, aligns one closer to the intention of Scripture.

- An eschatological sensibility of the Christian experience that begins with the End in mind, rooted in our present ascended identity "in Christ" in anticipation of our resurrected and deified future, a future absolutely certain because of Jesus' own resurrection and ascension (see 1 John 3:1–3).

The purpose of reading Scripture, from a patristic and "spiritual" perspective, is to glean from the facts of the literal-historical level the significance of what God has accomplished in the incarnation, of how "in Christ God was reconciling the world to himself" (2 Cor 5:19). "For the Fathers, the associative strategy" of identifying a multitude of tiny details clustered around the simplest, most straightforward passage "functioned like so many thin threads of connection between disparate portions of scripture."[8] By focusing on specific words and images in the Scripture, the Fathers collected pieces of the grand mosaic that allowed the image of Jesus, the Lion of Judah, to "stand forth" in the "written word" in a way that reveals his status as God's Eternal Word who gives all the particular words of Scripture their ultimate referent and meaning.

This book proposes that it is the way of *anagogy* that completes, perfects, and "explains" the fourfold typological method for

---

8. O'Keefe and Reno, *Sanctified Vision.*, 66.

interpretation used by the Fathers. The Fathers believed we "start with the End in mind" if we are to grasp the full scope of Jesus' identity as creation's *telos*, its goal. Both Scripture and the cosmos are pointing towards, and illumined by, the wedding feast of the Lamb and coming of the heavenly Jerusalem (Rev 3:12; 19:9; 21:2–10). The gospel, as the Fathers understood it, is not simply a multi-layered mystery of literal, figurative, and moral lessons. It is an "eternal gospel" that has, as its foundation, the extra-biblical referent of Jesus, the Alpha and the Omega. He is both the Lion of Judah (Rev 5:5) and the Lamb who is slain (Rev 5:6–12). He is the Prototype of Adam in the garden, as well as the mighty Warrior of the Apocalypse (Rev 1:16). The true spirit of the Bible is discovered, as Origen reminds us, only "through *Anagogy*. We must *ascend* above history" if the meaning of history is to be made clear.[9] Jesus must be known as "he who is coming again" if "he who died" and "he who is risen" is to be apprehended in his forsaken grandeur as our *mysterium fidei*.

Beginning from above—or from the End—may be counterintuitive to us but it was second nature for the Fathers. Everything in the Christian faith begins and ends for them in the Paschal mystery of Christ and of human divinization in union with it. It was the experience of the resurrection, in particular, that accounts for the enduring phenomenon of the Church. It was the impact of *anagogy* that gave rise to the worldwide proclamation of the gospel. An anagogical or eschatological imagination fueled everything they said and did. The early Church never forgot the eschatological nature of the Messiah. They discerned that his incarnation can be grasped only in concert with an appreciation of his identity as the Eternal Word. The Fathers, in other words, managed to hold together—by always "remembering the future"[10]—the "eternal gospel" of Jesus, apart from which the literal gospel about Jesus loses its divine and evangelical power.

---

9. Quoted in Lubac *History and Spirit*, 323, emphasis added.

10. This is a phrase made famous by the Orthodox theologian John Zizioulas in his works on the Trinity and the Church.

In the end, it is not enough simply to highlight the unity of the Scriptures and the perspicacious way in which the Fathers masterly expound upon the smallest detail to disclose the entire form of Christ. We must also deepen our own appreciation of the way in which they grounded their typological approach to the Bible in the grand theo-drama culminating in Christ's second coming. Just "as each object from the Old Testament was a sign," for the Fathers, "announcing the New, so each object of the New Testament is in turn a sign whose reality is found 'in the ages to come.'"[11] It is this second coming—and the new Jerusalem, the wedding feast of the Lamb, and adoration of the Lamb who is slain—that is anticipated, made present, and prophesied in all the books of the Bible. The Fathers "possessed the art of seeing the total form [of Christ and his mysteries] within individual forms [chapters, events, words, and even letters of the Bible] and bringing it to light within them."[12] But "the eternal gospel alone"—the gospel read from the perspective of *anagogy* (Jesus ascended, exalted, sitting at the Father's right hand, coming again in glory, and divinizing all things)—can "reveal . . . all that concerns the person of the Son of God, the mysteries that are proposed to us by his discourses as well as [all] the realities of which his actions were the figure."[13]

---

11. Lubac, *History and Spirit*, 248.

12. Balthasar, *Glory of the Lord*, 529.

13. Lubac, *History and Spirit*, 248.

4

The Whole Christ

Ecclesia as Corpus Tri-forme

JESUS OF NAZARETH IS the center and end of history. As the Eternal Word made flesh, he is also divine. In his incarnate humanity, he is the true Israelite, whose life-story recapitulates the story of Israel, redeeming Israel's unfaithfulness with his perfect faithfulness. As the Father's agent of creation and redemption, Jesus holds all things together in himself (Col 1:17), and when he is once again manifest to the world-at-large, he will "bring every deed into judgment, including every secret thing, whether it be good or evil" (Eccl 12:14). In patristic theology the work of Christ restores and even surpasses the original unity created in the garden of Eden. Seeing Jesus in this biocular way—as the Incarnate Word and as the Cosmic Christ—is an integral part of assimilating an anagogical vision of God's grace in the world into one's own life.

With this orientation in mind, we consider now the mystery of Christ under three different but interrelated and mutually interpreting aspects. The wording varies among the Fathers, but Saint Irenaeus typifies the tradition when he insists that the term "body of Christ" can be apprehended appropriately only in its threefold meaning as a *corpus tri-forme*.[1] By this, Irenaeus means that the

---

1. Balthasar has a robust appreciation of the multidimensional mystery of

34

mystery of Christ is a multidimensional, multiform, and contemporaneous phenomenon, at once human and divine. Christ is truly present in the Scriptures, the Eucharist, and the Church. Each of these is mystically, yet truly, the body of Christ, though in distinct and different ways. These different "bodies" of Christ presuppose and complement each other. They cannot be separated nor in any way opposed to one another. Together they manifest and make present the *total presence* of Jesus Christ. They do so in mutually reciprocal ways, and none of them individually or all together exhaust the mystery of him who is the only-begotten of God.

There is also a strictly Christological *corpus tri-forme* of Jesus that complements his presence in word, sacrament, and Church. This is Jesus as the Eternal Word, the Incarnate Word, and the Final Word of God. As Alpha, Incarnate Logos, and Omega, he pre-existed the creation of the world, "was incarnate of the Blessed Virgin, Mary," and "will come again in glory" to present to the Father the recapitulated cosmos he has obtained for him. Here we see his Christological *tri-forme* in a certain anagogical light: he is the Pre-existent Word, the Incarnate Word, and the *Totus Christus* (Total Christ)—the Corporate Christ—who has reconciled and incorporated "all things in himself" (Col 1:20; cf. Rom 11:36) to the end that "God may be all in all" (1 Cor 15:28).

These varying forms of the *corpus tri-forme* "are intertwined with one another and overlap" and are "perceptible expressions" of the single Word, Jesus Christ.[2] They give witness to the fact that Jesus is able to establish *multiple presences of himself*, whole and entire, across the full breadth of the economy of salvation. He does so for the glory and honor of his Father, and for the deifying assimilation of the members of his body into the life of the Trinity. There is an organic unfolding of the one body of Christ in a multiplicity of "incarnational forms" throughout history.

---

the "body of Christ" as and extension of his incarnation in word, sacrament, and Church. For an extensive treatment of Balthasar's vision in this regard, see Mongrain, *Systematic Thought of Hans Urs von Balthasar*, 37–39. See also Krill and McCullough, *Life in the Trinity*, 46–56.

2. Mongrain, *Systematic Thought of Hans Urs von Balthasar*, 38.

Jesus' incarnation can be seen—as it was by the Fathers—as a temporally extended body, including both old and new covenants. Saint Gregory Nazianzus agrees with Saint Irenaeus that God exercised a certain *paideia*—pedagogical patience—in introducing his Son into the world. The Fathers envisioned a Trinitarian structure of history that recognized "it was imprudent, while the Father was not yet acknowledged as [the only] God, to announce the Son openly; and, as long as the divinity of the Son had not yet been accepted, to speak of the Holy Spirit."[3] The writings of the Old Testament have been included in the canon by the Church because they testify to "the first phase" of the narrative of Christ's incarnation. Yet, even the record of the New Testament, including the Paschal mystery, constitutes only a "second phase" of the Word-become-flesh. The *fullness* of Christ's presence in the world is "enfleshed" (incarnated) in the development of the Church (both as a community of charisms and as an institution), particularly its eucharistic worship. The mystery of the incarnation, then, "is a cumulative process that can only be adequately understood if it is seen in its historical totality as the redemptive work of the Trinity in history."[4]

Positing Jesus to be the one *from whom* all Scripture and history proceeds and *to whom* all Scripture and history leads, we now undertake to illustrate how this same Eternal Word of God—"incarnate" in the Scriptural record—finds his fuller "incarnation" in the Eucharist and, even more completely, in the *Ecclesia de Eucharistia*. If the incarnation of Christ is a dynamic, historically encompassing event referring to the way in which Jesus and his Holy Spirit (as the "two hands of God," in Saint Irenaeus' phrase) are recapitulating and recreating the world for the Father, then the *corpus mysticum* of Christ—understood as his mystical body, both as Eucharist and as Church—is the linchpin in this dynamic process. Called the *triplex modus corporis*, the eucharistic and ecclesial "bodies" of Christ are mystical

---

3. Balthasar, *Theo-Logic*, 200n47, quoting Saint Gregory Nazianzus, *Orations* 31, 26–27. Balthasar notes also that there are hints of this account already in Irenaeus, *Against Heresies* IV.20.5.

4. Mongrain, *Systematic Thought of Hans Urs von Balthasar*, 38.

extensions of his historical incarnation. These "mystical bodies of Christ" must not be seen as in any way "less real" than the historical Jesus witnessed to in the Scripture. On the contrary, seen from an anagogical perspective, they constitute the divinely intended plenitude and purpose of his incarnation.

For those who are used to thinking of the Church as an institution that has sacraments, it can be difficult to acquire an understanding of the Church as a sacrament that also has institutions. Still more difficult for us to grasp, perhaps, is the theological fact that the Church is Jesus himself. The *Ecclesia* is the fullness (*pleroma*) of his incarnate mystery. Here, in a way that both darkens yet illuminates human reason, Jesus incorporates his members into his own *corpus mysticum* until such time as his body "comes to full stature" or "is brought to completion" (Eph 4:13). This is the mystery of what Saint Augustine's calls *Totus Christus* (the total Christ).[5]

Once our vision becomes accustomed to Christ's *corpus triforme*, we can see more clearly that Christianity is not merely a "religion of the book."[6] It is, rather, an ongoing encounter with the Risen Lord who incorporates his people into himself. This incorporation is at once axiological (vertical, divine) and diachronic (historical, human). It is an anagogical mystery actualized in word and sacrament because the drama of our salvation—the Paschal mystery—transcends time, even though it a series of events that occurred at very specific moments in time. Because it is a *theandric* (divine-human) action, it can thus be *made present* wherever and whenever the memorial bequeathed by Jesus to his apostles is enacted according to his command (Luke 22:19). "All that was in (the historical Jesus) Christ has passed over into his mysteries," as

---

5. "Let us rejoice then and give thanks that we have become not only Christians, but Christ himself. Do you understand and grasp, brethren, God's grace toward us? Marvel and rejoice: we have become Christ. For if he is the head, we are the members; he and we together are the whole man. . . . The fullness of Christ then is the head and the members. But what does 'head and members' mean? Christ and the Church." Augustine, *In Johannis evangelium* 21, 8, quoted in CCC 795n230. See also, CCC 1136.

6. CCC 108.

DEIFYING VISION

Saint Pope Leo the Great put it,[7] and this mystical apprehension is reiterated by the *Catechism of the Catholic Church* when it states:

> In the liturgy of the Church, it is principally his own Paschal mystery that Christ signifies and makes present. During his earthly life, Jesus announced his Paschal mystery by his teaching and anticipated it by his actions. When his Hour comes, he lives out the unique event of history which does not pass away: Jesus dies, is buried, rises from the dead, and is seated at the right hand of the Father "once for all." His Paschal mystery is a real event that occurred in our history, but it is unique: all other historical events happen once, and then they pass away, swallowed up in the past. The Paschal mystery of Christ, by contrast, cannot remain only in the past, because by his death he destroyed death, and all that Christ is—all that he did and suffered for all men—participates in the divine eternity, and so transcends all times while being made present in them all. The event of the Cross and Resurrection abides and draws everything toward life.[8]

Drawing everything toward life. "I, when I am lifted up from the earth, will draw all men to myself" (John 12:32).[9] Indwelling these truths, seeing Christian faith and experience in and through them, is what the anagogical imagination is all about.

Participating in the liturgy, then, is key to understanding and experiencing the tri-form fullness of Jesus as the Incarnate Word of God. Christ's presence in Scripture finds its fullest expression in his sacramental actions, just as his miracles testify to the truth about Jesus more profoundly than do his moral teachings. Actions speak louder than words, presentation impacts more than description. The Word of God (Jesus) in Scripture finds its fulfillment in the Word of God (Jesus) as Eucharist. The Bible testifies to the priority of the liturgy (Luke 22:19; cf. 1 Cor 11:24), even as

7. CCC 1115.

8. CCC 1085.

9. The Greek literally rendered reads "will draw all to myself," which is generally completed as "all men" or "all things." The ambiguity the Greek text can be seen as underscoring a wide scope of God's redemptive purposes in Christ.

38

the liturgy incorporates and embodies the Scripture. The Eucharist makes "present and real" the content (Jesus) of what the word records, while the written and preached word supplies a fullness of understanding in the sacramental event that it does not have on its own. Everything in the Christian world leads to and from this eucharistic mystery.

Seen from this perspective, the narrative of our salvation acquires an even more dramatic form. Recall that soteriology (doctrine of salvation) must be reconceived, not as God's response to a fallen world, but as the fallen world conceived for the incarnation. Can we not see revealed here a more beautifully bewildering truth? For if the world was created for the incarnation, can we not say further that the incarnation was created for the mystery of the Eucharist? And the mystery of the Eucharist for the mystery of the Church? This is the vision of the early Church, as well as that of the fathers of the Vatican II Council.[10] The *corpus tri-forme* of Jesus includes his incarnation as a human, the mystical extension of his presence in the Eucharist, and the anagogical inclusion of the world in himself through his Church. Word and sacrament in liturgy are the middle term in the *corpus tri-forme* of the *Totus Christus*.

Recall also how, according to Saint Irenaeus, Jesus came into the world as its Savior, *but only because the Father had created a world that needed saving for his merciful Son.* The Son, in turn, bequeaths his disciples the mystery of his Eucharist, creating simultaneously the corporate assembly of those who would be gathered unto his heart. Yet, all of these creations and recreations find as their co-mission the redemption of what has been lost, the deliverance of what has been enslaved. The *economia* is the record of the redemptive work of the Trinity throughout history, and the *corpus tri-forme* of Jesus as Scripture, sacrament, and Church is the prime instrument of this Trinitarian work. Yet, the cult of the

10. For an introduction to the *Communio* ecclesiology that both inspired and flowed from the great Catholic liturgists and theologians who influenced Vatican II, see Paul McPartlan, "*Ressourcement*, Vatican II, and Eucharistic Ecclesiology," in Flynn and Murray, *Ressourcement*, 392–404.

Church serves the *economia*, not vice versa. Jesus came for the life of the *world*, not for the life of the Church. The Church is not a club. It is an instrument of the mission of God. The incarnation creates the Eucharist, and the Eucharist creates the Church. But Scripture, Eucharist, and Church serve the anagogical purposes of Father, Son, and Holy Spirit.

From this "economic" perspective, the Church must be regarded as "the Sacrament of Salvation."[11] The story of the Church is the story of the new people of God. The Eucharist makes the Church, and the Church instantiates the Eucharist. It is the Church, as both the outcome and the extension of the mystery of the Eucharist, that advances the dramatic narrative of the Trinitarian re-creation of the world.

We must note again the *proleptic* relationship of Scripture to itself. "The New Testament is hidden in the Old," said Saint Augustine, "and the Old is manifest in the New."[12] The Old is surpassed without becoming redundant or irrelevant to the New that has come. With the patristic concept of Christ's *corpus tri-forme*, we have seen a similar dynamic: the incarnation, as well as its scriptural record in both Old and New Testaments, contains the seeds of the Eucharist, while the institution and celebration of the Eucharist by Jesus' and his disciples perfects and fulfills the intent and meaning of the incarnation. These phenomena are oriented to the creation of Christ's *Ecclesia*. The Church is the earthly *pleroma* of those gathered into Christ through the exercise of his word and sacrament. "The Church is the goal of all things."[13]

At the same time, the Church is the body (1 Cor 12:12) and bride of Christ (2 Cor 11:2). He is as hypostatically united with her as he is with Father and Spirit in the Trinity. We have seen how from the very beginning Jesus is never alone. "Not-aloneness"

11. For a treatment of how the Church is not an institution that has sacraments, but a sacrament that employs institutions to carry out its effects, see McPartlan, *Sacrament of Salvation*.

12. *Quaestiones in Heptateuchum* 2, 73 (PL 34, 623), cited in McPartlan, *Sacrament of Salvation*, 14. Cf. CCC 129; *Dei Verbum* 16.

13. CCC 760.

defines the very nature of God. Thus, from all eternity—prior to the *economia* and his coming among us in his incarnation—Jesus "indwells" the Father and the Father "indwells" the Son. They do so (in the words of Chalcedon) "without change and without confusion." "In the beginning was the Word. The Word was with God and the Word was God" (John 1:1). His identity is forever inseparable a part of a "we." "I" and "Thou" in the Trinity defines the nature of God. Father and Son are never not together. God is never not Trinity. Jesus is never not united: first from all eternity with his Father and their Holy Spirit in the immanent Trinity, then in the incarnation with his mother, Mary.

Jesus' "never aloneness" also defines his relationship with the world and his Church. His incarnation continues and makes visible the "connectedness" and "inseparability" from "the other" that defines his nature as God. As the Word-made-flesh Jesus is also never alone. From the moment of his conception he is linked inseparable with Mary. He is the member of a family with several "brothers and sisters" (Mark 6:3; cf. Matt 12:50; 19:29). Saint Paul describes him as "the firstborn of many brethren" (Rom 8:29). He identifies himself often with "the least of my brethren" (Matt 25:40–45). He does what he does because he is who he is: the Son of the Father and the brother of all men and women. His very identity, both as God and man, is one of absolute relatedness. He is the only-begotten Son of the Father and the all-encompassing Redeemer of the human family. Thus, he is also the Head of his body, the Church (Eph 5:23), the Cornerstone of all creation (Luke 20:17; Eph 2:20). "Everything that was made was made for him" (Rom 11:36) and there "is nothing that is made that is not" intended for communion with and fulfillment in and through him (cf. John 1:3).

These Christological convictions of Christian faith shed light, in an anticipatory way (using a "hermeneutic of faith"), on the Old Testament allusions to Jesus as the Messiah and as a *corporate personality*. The Old Testament prepares us to recognize Jesus not only as "the Promised of Ages," but also as a divine-human figure who is able to embody and enact the mysterious plan of the Father "to unite all things in himself, things in heaven and things on earth" (Eph 1:10). We see this perspective on Jesus develop gradually in the prophetic writings. Ezekiel, for example, is made by God "a symbol for the house of Israel" (Ezek 12:6). God commands Ezekiel to manifest in his own person both the sins and consequences of sin that pertain to God's people (Ezek 3:22–27). Jeremiah receives similar commands (Jer 13:1–11). These prophets do not simply announce the impending judgment of God, they *exhibit it* and even help initiate the catastrophes they foretell. We begin to see in Ezekiel a figure who serves the people as a *summation and surrogate* for what ails and awaits them.

Two other dramatic figures in prophetic literature also point the way to Jesus as the Messiah who is also a *corpus tri-forme*. The first is a figure and a title Jesus uses to identify himself: "the Son of Man." We learn about the Son of Man most powerfully in the book of Daniel (7:9–14). Here he is described as an individual figure who is "given dominion and glory and kingdom, that all peoples, nations, and languages should serve him" and whose "dominion is an everlasting dominion, which shall not pass away, and his kingdom shall never be destroyed." At the same time, "the saints of the Most High shall receive the kingdom, and possess the kingdom forever, forever and ever," implying that this triumphant Son of Man is somehow an inclusive figure, and individual who incorporates and embodies the multitude for salvation.

Jesus appropriates this corporate sense of himself as the Son of Man several times in the New Testament. In his description of the last judgment, for example, he identifies himself with every other human person who has ever lived (Matt 25:31–46). Again, and perhaps more memorably, in his teaching on the Eucharist, Jesus insists, "Unless you eat the flesh of the Son of Man and drink his blood, you have no life in you; he who eats my flesh and drinks my blood has eternal life, and I will raise him up on the last day" (John 6:53–54).

Does Saint Paul have these sayings of Jesus in mind when he tells the Colossians that their real life is "hidden with God in Christ" (Col 3:3)? Or when he tells them, "When Christ is revealed [as the Son of Man] . . . you too will be revealed in all your glory with him" (Col 3:1–4)? More than any theologian before or since, Saint Paul had a living sense of Jesus as a corporate personality. No doubt this stemmed in part from his encounter with the Risen Lord on the road to Damascus: "Saul, Saul, why are you persecuting me?" (Acts 9:4). Who is the "me" that Jesus is talking about here? His Church, of course: his body, without whom the Lord himself is, in some sense, incomplete. It is in the mystical vision of Saint Paul that we catch our best glimpse of the reality of Jesus as the *corpus mysticum*: Head with members, glorifying God, as a single mystery, the *Totus Christus*.

When combined with the eucharistic identification with the Son of Man noted above, we can begin to envision how Jesus as a corporate person can give us his mystical body (*corpus mysticum*)—both as Eucharist and as Church—to incorporate into himself all those "predestined before the foundation of the world" to be united with him in glory. In so doing, he fulfills the Old Testament prophecy that God's Faithful Servant would be established as the "light of the nations" (Isa 42:6; 49:6), receiving "whole nations for his tribute" (Isa 53:12), and bringing the Father's salvation "to the ends of the earth" (Isa 49:6). As Paul McPartlan has said, "The Old Testament can be said to spiral in towards Christ . . . as the faithful people [of Israel] progressively diminish in number *until only one persons stands at the focal point* [namely, Jesus] . . . and it spirals out from Christ as new people in new places are increasingly gathered into the new people of God."[14]

We have now come full circle. The all-inclusive Trinity creates our world so that the world might be incorporated into Christ. The promises made to Abraham that "in you all the families of earth would be blessed" (Gal 3:8; cf.) are now fulfilled in and by Jesus Christ. He alone is the Faithful One whose fidelity to the commands and expectations of the covenant made by his Father with Israel never falters. Beginning in his incarnation, he calls men and women into his company as disciples. With his death, resurrection, and ascension, and through the sacramental mysteries he bequeaths to his Church, he extends his summons

---

14. McPartlan, *Sacrament of Salvation*, 22; emphasis added.

to communion with himself to the ends of the earth. He is no longer content simply to make disciples among the nations; he desires to create a new family for his heavenly Father, of whom he is both Head and Bridegroom. The preparation of the children of Abraham, which is the story of the Old Testament, comes to perfection in the birth of Christ: first in his incarnation, then in his *corpus mysticum* (both as Eucharist and Church). The fullness of Christ is accomplished only when God has put all enemies under his feet (1 Cor 15:25) and all things have found their rightful place in him. How beautifully Saint Paul expresses the incorporative and recapitulative mission of Jesus when he says: "When all things are subjected to him, then the Son himself will also be subjected to him who put all things under him, that God may be everything to every one" (1 Cor 15:28). Saint John the Evangelist envisioned where all anagogy leads when, exiled on Patmos, saw "the holy city, new Jerusalem, coming down out of heaven from God, prepared as a bride adorned for her husband" (Rev 21:2). In this heavenly city, Jesus alone is the Light (Rev 21:23). All his member saints are seated with him as the *Christus Totus* at the wedding feast of the Lamb (Rev 19:19). He remains forever among them "as the Lamb who is slain" (Rev 5:12).

5

Eschaton as Restoration

Now and Not Yet

> See what love the Father has given us, that we should
> be called children of God; and so we are. The reason
> why the world does not know us is that it did not
> know him. Beloved, we are God's children now; it
> does not yet appear what we shall be, but we know
> that when he appears we shall be like him, for we
> shall see him as he is. (1 John 3:1–2)

AN ANAGOGICAL SENSE OF Scripture, doctrine, and of life can enable Christians to grasp the promised glory of the final consummation made to our forebears in the faith. Salvation history is realized
ultimately, and most fully, in the wedding feast of the Lamb.

It is helpful to maintain the sweep of salvation history before
us. Abraham's posterity were formed into a chosen people following the exodus by a covenant sealed with blood (Exod 29:21).
They were given law and land and promised that a universal
communion would be theirs (Gen 15:5; cf. Mal 3:12). Jerusalem
became their capital and Torah and the temple secured their
identity. Despite political and religious upheavals, prophets like
Jeremiah foretold a new exodus (Jer 23:7–8) enjoining a new covenant and a more comprehensive law (Jer 31:31–34). Isaiah and
Zechariah envisioned a universal gathering that would require a

new (supernatural) Jerusalem and temple to accommodate it (Isa 66:18–23; Zech 8:22–23). The mission of God and the mission of Israel are the same: restoring the cosmos to its original unity with the Father of all, and in Jesus these promises are realized. Jesus is the new law, the new Moses, the new temple. He completes what has gone before, while simultaneously validating and sanctifying the promises and practices peculiar to Israel. The scandal of his cross becomes the catalyst and linchpin for the creation of his kingdom. The eucharistic Church—*Ecclesia de Eucharistia*—is Jesus himself, gathering all nations to his Father in a way prepared for by, yet exceeding, "the promises made to Abraham and his children forever" (Luke 1:55).

It is important to note that the promises made to Abraham, embodied and amplified in the successive covenants made with the chosen people of Israel, are fulfilled in Jesus *forsaken*. They come to fruition, in other words, through the *self-expropriation* of this *crucified* King. The culmination of salvation history occurs through God's *kenosis* in Christ (cf. Phil 2:6–11). *Salvation is cruciform*. This is a core truth of both the Trinitarian and the Christological mysteries.[1] This fact introduces an element of suspense into the drama of redemption. An "already-not yet" eschatological tension characterizes all reflection on the coming of the kingdom of God.[2] The kingdom of God is inaugurated and definitively established by Jesus in his incarnation and his Paschal mystery, yet it awaits his second coming "in glory" for its final consummation. All theological and liturgical reflection revolves around these two foci, and this is what the anagogical sense of Scripture points us toward and keeps before us.

The story of the new people of God—the new Israel of Jesus that includes, transforms, perfects, and fulfills the old Israel of "our forebears in the faith"—is the narrative of an ever-expanding, catholic

---

1. For its Trinitarian expression, see Balthasar, *Theo-Drama*, IV, esp., 317–32. For its Christological expression, see Gorman, *Inhabiting the Cruciform God*, 105–28.

2. Gorman describes this tension as a "participative anticipation" in *Inhabiting the Cruciform God*, 162–70. For a general summary of Catholic eschatology, see CCC 668–77, 763.

fullness that stretches over two thousand years in three basic steps: the incarnation, the eucharistic mystery, the *Ecclesia de Eucharistia*. As the instrument of the salvation and redemption he embodied and imparted to a fallen world, Jesus assumed our human nature in his incarnation and bequeathed to us the supernatural memorial of his person and work in the mystery of the Eucharist. His Eucharist, in turn, together with its twin mysteries of Holy Baptism and Sacred Chrismation, creates, sustains, and grows his Church. The Lord's ecclesial body is one with him, members and Head. Christ's Church is also his bride. It is for his Church—both body and bride—that Jesus intentionally surrendered his life (Eph 5:25). Purchased with the blood of the Lamb (Acts 20:28; Rev 5:9), the *Ecclesia de Eucharistia* is the earthly aim and end of Jesus' advent and incarnation among us as the Word-made-flesh.

But even the creation of the Church is penultimate to what God in Christ is doing for the world through the power of his Holy Spirit. To be sure, the Church is the sacrament of Reconciliation.[3] It is the efficacious sign and instrument of inclusion in the Son's divine person and mission. As such it is also our *salvation*, for salvation is nothing other than assimilation and insertion into the life of the Trinity, conjoined there through the person and work of Jesus, the Son. Again "all that was in Jesus" has passed over into us, just as "what was visible in our Savior has passed over into his mysteries."[4] It is through the Church, the *Ur-sakrament* (source/primordial sacrament), most especially the sacraments of initiation, that the deifying life of the Trinity is communicated to his holy people. All seven sacraments (as the Catholic Church observes) are as provisional as the *Ecclesia* that contains and provides them, for:

---

3. "Whether it aids the world or whether it benefits from it, the Church has but one sole purpose—that the kingdom of God may come and the salvation of the human race may be accomplished. Every benefit the people of God can confer on mankind during its earthly pilgrimage is rooted in the Church's being 'the universal sacrament of salvation,' at once manifesting and actualizing the mystery of God's love for men." Vatican II, *Gaudium et Spes*, 45.

4. Leo the Great, *Sermon* 74, 2, in CCC 1115.

The church lives in the overlap of the ages with its spiritual eyes constantly focused on both the past event of Christ's death, resurrection, and exaltation and the future event of Christ's *parousia* and God's redemption of creation. Life together in and for the world is determined by these two great divine interventions in human history, as we live in the overlap between this age and the age to come.[5]

Both Church and her sacraments will reach their anagogical fulfillment when the kingdom of God appears complete. They will give way to a new reality, the new Jerusalem (Rev 3:12; 21:2). This "heavenly bride" descending from above bears some resemblance to its sacramental anticipations on earth, but far surpasses and supersedes what we see of her today. The second coming of Christ is the new dawn, rendering the candle light of the *Ecclesia de Eucharistia* no longer needed.

As the divine "Gatherer," Jesus is the power of God completing the mission of God. He comes to "gather all the things into himself" (Col 1:16–17). This is the purpose for which the promise of unlimited descendants was made to Abraham (Gen 1:18; 22:18). The wedding at Cana, the parable of the prodigal son, the encounter of the woman at Jacob's well: all of these "new testaments" of God's salvific action in Christ bear witness to "the process by which Jesus gathers to himself a bride."[6] If our first parents' fall from grace can be characterized as a shattering and dispersion, our restoration in Christ can be seen as the persistent and indefatigable re-collection—the gathering—of the lost (tribes, sheep, etc.) back to the Father who made them for perfect happiness in communion with himself. Our infidelities inhibit but are ultimately no obstacle to God the Gatherer. Covenants are re-crafted time and again in the history preceding the coming of Christ in an attempt to get God's hard-hearted people to believe the good news of their divine election (e.g., Jer 31:31; Ezek 11:19). Hence, the author of Hebrews concludes: "Long ago God spoke to our ancestors in many and

---

5. Gorman, *Reading Paul*, 185–86.
6. Barron, *Priority of Christ*, 83.

various ways by the prophets, but in these last days he has spoken to us by a Son, whom he appointed heir of all things, through whom he also created the worlds" (Heb 1:1–2). The miracles Jesus worked, the parables he told, the transformational encounters he had with distinct individuals—each of these, in its own unique manner, gives testimony to the magnetic mission of Jesus in his incarnation. He is sent with the express purpose of gathering the lost tribes of Israel—and through them, the remainder of the fallen cosmos—back into perfect communion with the Father. The Church continues the *missio Dei* in word, sacrament, and charitable action. It is a mission, moreover, that will continue until the body of Christ "comes to full stature" (Eph 4:13), a mystery that coincides with God being "all in all" (Eph 4:6).

Christians, then, are caught up into the symphonic sweep of this eschatological vision by way of *anagogy*. Anagogy enables one to view the present through the lens of the future, a vision of life on earth from the perspective of eternity. It is a vision of the *Ecclesia de Eucharistia* driven by an apprehension shared by the communion of saints in heaven. It is a liturgically oriented sensibility derived from a contemplative apprehension of the heavenly liturgy and of the wedding feast of the Lamb. It is an *eschatological* sense of things, one in which the tension between the "already" and "not yet" of God's kingdom is purposely made more acute in order to generate a renewed sense of the early Christian plea, "*Maranatha*. Amen! Come, Lord Jesus!" (Rev 22:20).

Anagogia, the pull of all things upwards into Christ, is to the *economia* (the outward working of salvation history as recorded in Scripture) what the ascension is to the incarnation. Jesus' resurrected body was at once continuous and discontinuous with his crucified flesh. "Put your fingers in my wounds," he tells Thomas, "doubt no longer but believe" (John 20:27). "It is the Lord!" John exclaims to Peter, recognizing Jesus on the seashore after his resurrection (John 21:7). In all his resurrection manifestations, Jesus was clearly recognizable in his glorified body by those who knew him in the flesh. He even took meals with his disciples, demonstrating to them his identity with the man they knew prior to his

crucifixion and burial (Luke 24:39). At the same time, he was altogether different. "Do not touch me," he says to Mary Magdalene.
"I have not yet ascended to my Father and your Father" (John
20:17). His glorified body can pass through walls. It can appear
and disappear. There seems to be an inherent ambivalence and
delayed response in those who finally recognize the risen Christ
as the very same Jesus they knew before. Jesus' resurrection completes but transcends his incarnation. *Anagogy* does the same for
the whole of salvation history. *Anagogy* is, so to say, a perspective of eschatological *Aufheben*: a superior, transcendent vision
that gathers up, re-collects, distills, and illumines all the narrative
pieces of the drama of our redemption.[7]

---

7. Balthasar makes much of the concept of *Aufheben*, connecting its gathering, sublating, and synthetically perfecting power to the Trinitarian perichoresis and Jesus' redemption of the world by "gathering all things unto Himself."
Balthasar, *Theo-Drama*, V, 411.

6

Life Ascending

Anagogy as Mystagogy

IN HIS DISCUSSION OF the Cappadocian contribution to the development of the Church's doctrine of Christ, Brian Daley effectively summarizes much of the thrust of this project:

> To learn how to interpret the various things in the Scriptures that are said of Christ, to meditate on each event in the life of Jesus as something that involves us in his passage to life through the world of death, is a discipline that eventually will enable us to "look at and be looked at by God" [quoting Saint Gregory of Nazianzus], to "ascend with his Godhead and no longer remain among visible things, but be raised up to the intelligible realm, and know what is said of his nature, what of his saving incarnation." So at the end of his "Fourth Theological Oration," after briefly commenting on the various Scriptural titles of Christ, . . . Gregory concludes:
>
> > These are the titles of the Son. Walk through those of them that are lofty in a way befitting of God, and through the bodily ones with compassion—or rather, walk through all of them divinely, so that you may become God, rising up from

below through the one who for our sake came
down from above.

To know the full Mystery of Christ, "'the same yesterday
and today' in bodily form, and spiritually 'for all ages,'" is
already to share in what that Mystery promises.[1]

Letter leading to spirit. Spirit transforming humanity. Mystery inviting participation. Participation facilitating assimilation. Man becoming divine. That last phrase of course is the kind of bald, and to many shocking, expressions found among the Fathers of the early Church, which is typically referred to as divinization or deification. Daley's outline of the patristic assumptions behind biblical reading, however, accurately summarize the process that this volume seeks to reanimate in our own day, of deifying vision. This is the anagogical way as practiced by the ecclesial and monastic Fathers and Mothers and promoted in their teaching. What we see in such passages is anagogy as mystagogy.

Mystagogy is associated primarily with teaching regarding the mysteries, that is, the sacraments. Famous texts along these lines would be the mystagogical treatises of Cyril of Jerusalem, Gregory of Nyssa, and Maximus the Confessor. But fundamentally, mystagogy means training in or leading into mystery, and mystery is a frequent word in the biblical and patristic vocabulary of the whole Christian experience of redemption and encounter with God. Jesus speaks of the disciples' privileged access to the "mystery of the kingdom of God" (Mark 4:11). Saint Paul speaks of the mystery of God's will revealed in Jesus and in the Church's participation in the person of Jesus (Eph 2:4–7), and in the "mystery of our religion" (1 Tim 3:16). The gospel is experienced as a mystery, according to the New Testament, because the world is under a kind of veil, a spiritual concealment due to its hardness of heart, blinding it from the truth about God (2 Cor 3:14–16).

The spiritual sense of Scripture, of which anagogy is a part, is that which illuminates the mystery of the gospel, particularly in its personally transformative dimensions. As has been argued in this project, reviving an awareness of the anagogical sense of Scripture

1. Daley, *God Visible*, 137.

revives the anagogical sense of life. Jesus is no longer perceived as "up there" while we're "down here" trying our best to imitate him and hoping God is pleased with our efforts. We increasingly see in the light of anagogy that we have already been brought "up there" in Christ, he lives "down here" with us; we experience the presence of the kingdom *now* in our lives and in the Church even as we grieve the "not yet" obscurity of the kingdom awaiting its fullness at the end of time. In all of this, our lives are "hidden" in Christ (Col 3:3), an enigma and oddity—a mystery—to the onlooking world and sometimes even to ourselves.

Doctrinal *Anagōgē*

Among the points of Christian doctrine that contribute to our knowledge and therefore our progress in spiritual formation, four are representative and serve to effectively illuminate the anagogical dimensions of gospel.

Filiation is a Latin term meaning to be made into a son. It is a repeated theme in the New Testament that those "in Christ" are no longer mere servants of God but are sons of God by virtue of union with the Son of God. Many Christians, however, perceive themselves and live their lives almost exclusively in the servant category. And good servants they are. But they hesitate to embrace a deeper dimension of relationship with God. The way of anagogy leads upwards toward this deeper, more intimate relationship with God. In filiation, servanthood is caught up into sonship and all the familial and beneficial implications associated with this status.

Some today chafe at the masculine implications of "sonship" and prefer the label of "child of God." The identity of "child" is a true one and validated by Scripture. But sonship carries with it the close identification with the Son and the elevated status (especially in traditional cultures) that the term implies. The point is that Christians are the beneficiaries and inheritors of all of God's promises since the time of Abraham. It is this expansive, inclusive sense of sonship that is communicated in the term.

Deification has already been discussed, and while the term *theosis* or its cognates does not occur in the New Testament, the raw material of the concept can be found. "To be made God" is the way the Church Father's spoke of becoming "partakers in the divine nature" (2 Pet 1:4). It is a doctrine also derived from the transfiguration, the episode in the story of Jesus and one that not only has there-and-then significance in salvation history but here-and-now implications for Christian identity. What was true of Jesus' humanity will be true of ours—we will glow with divine permeation. The accounts of saints whose bodies resist corruption and who in death appear beautiful and even smell unlike corpses are all part of this heritage of the transformation—the transfiguration—of humanity-in-Christ. The doctrine of deification can serve to elevate the perspective of the Christian experience from the merely moral to the ontological—our very mode of existence is being "changed from glory to glory" (2 Cor 3:18).

Unification is the longing of the Son of God for all God's people. From his heartfelt lamentation over Jerusalem, whose chicks he would gather in his arms, to his great prayer before his trial (John 17), Jesus desires his people to be "one." This is translated in Saint Paul into eschatological terms, that is, a present reality awaiting full manifestation. Unification is an important dimension of the gospel for a culture like ours that disproportionately emphasizes the individual dimension of human existence. Our personhood, our existence as a one-of-a-kind instantiation of human being, is never denied in Scripture. But what is in Scripture, and recognized in liturgical theology especially, is our existence as a *corporate personality*. The Church is a corporate body identifying itself under a singular feminine pronoun. Saint Paul of course deploys anatomical metaphors by which to describe the working of this body of Christ made up of many members. We who are many are one. It calls upon an anagogical imagination to overcome the insistent individualism of Western culture and the reduction of our existence to the merely singular.

Finally there is the anticipation of *cosmic restoration* which the anagogical sense of Scripture promotes and informs. The

Greek word *apokatastasis* has recently assumed a new and elevated profile in New Testament studies.[2] The word occurs once, where Saint Peter preaches about "the Christ appointed for you, Jesus, whom heaven must receive until the time for *establishing* all that God spoke by the mouths of his holy prophets from of old" (Acts 3:21). The New Revised Standard Version translates this as "the time of *universal restoration* that God announced long ago." The New Testament, drawing on imagery found in the Old Testament, anticipates "a new heaven and a new earth" (2 Pet 3:13; cf. Isa 66:22). Like deification, the hope of cosmic restoration raises the understanding of the Christian experience from one of merely waiting for "heaven when you die" to that of a complete transformation of all things, the deification of all things, if you will, when in Saint Paul's words "God will be all in all" (1 Cor 15:28; Eph 1:22).

When seen in this light, the entire New Testament can be understood as a gigantic *anagogy* of the Old Testament, bringing the promises to the patriarchs and people of Israel to their anticipated and now revealed purposes. All things are caught up into God's redemptive intentions in his Son, by his Spirit (John 12:32). Perceiving oneself, and *believing* oneself, to be caught up into these cosmic-transfiguring intentions is what the anagogical sense of Scripture is all about.

Active *Anagōgē*

There are many ways of mapping one's progress in spiritual formation, but among the Church Fathers whom we have been focusing on one way stands out among them all. Saint Maximus the Confessor in *The Four Hundred Chapters on Love* outlines this way in a casual reference when he writes: "The virtues separate the mind

2. *Apokatastasis* serves as a focal term in recent studies of what is termed "universal salvation" by scholars seeking to recover a theme intimated in the New Testament and articulated by some patristic era theologians. This retrieval project is not without controversy. Representative texts include Ramelli, *Larger Hope?*; Hart, *That All Shall Be Saved*.

from the passions; spiritual contemplations separate it from simple representations; then pure prayer sets it before God himself."[3]

Virtues, contemplation, pure prayer. Saint Maximus here alludes to the form of monastic spirituality known as the Threefold Way, first developed among the Desert Fathers and Mothers of the third and fourth centuries who withdrew to the deserts principally in Egypt. The theology, psychology, and practices of these monastics are preserved in their sayings and particularly transmitted in the writing of Evagrius of Pontus, who lived between 345 to 399. The classic text in this regards is *The Praktikos* ("Practice"), an example of what is called "ascetical theology," that is, an account of how one increasingly disposes oneself toward full union with God. The Threefold Way is a distillation of profound experience and diligent practice, an encounter with representative texts can educe a sense of conviction for the intensity of self-preoccupation, creature comfort, and status-consciousness with which Christians today are surrounded and by which they are deeply influenced.[4]

While diagrammed as a three-stage progression and helpful as such, the Threefold Way is also an analysis of the different dimensions of the Christian life one oscillates back and forth between. One is never completely through with the first stage, no matter of far along one has progressed, and the Christian lives of some saints began in the "mystical" experience of the third stage, which introduced them to the initial step of Christian conversion and salvation.

Labeled in a variety of ways, the Threefold Way is composed of *purgation* (or *purification*), *illumination*, and *perfection* (or *unification*)—the purgative, illuminative, and unitive ways. The purgative stage, as the label suggests, addresses those things that

---

3. Maximus the Confessor, *Selected Writings*, 67.

4. The classic text is *The Praktikos*, found in Evagrius Ponticus, *Praktikos and Chapters on Prayer*; see also Ward, *Desert Fathers*; Diogenes Allen provides a very helpful and accessible introduction to the Threefold Way in *Spiritual Theology*; Thomas Keating outlines the three stages as depicted in the lives of Martha, Mary, and Lazarus in *The Better Part*, and Ralph Martin provides an accessible contemporary application of the Threefold Way in *The Fulfillment of All Desire*. For an integration of the Threefold Way and contemporary Christian psychology, see Shults and Sandage, *Transforming Spirituality*, 26–36.

hinder progress in spiritual formation. Here one thinks of Saint Paul's characteristic lists of vices such as found in Gal 5:18–21 and Col 3:5–10. The desert monastics drew particular attention to an analysis of what they identified as "passions" or thoughts that bedeviled the monks (or anyone serious about progress in faith) and obstructed their inner freedom. These passions or thoughts, eight in number, form the basis of the more familiar Western analysis of the seven deadly sins. In the original itera-tion, these passions or thoughts (identified as such because the monks were not as concerned about discrete acts that one might commit as the way in which these vices of habitual preoccupa-tion hindered spiritual formation) were, in the Evagrian order, gluttony, impurity, greed, sadness, anger, *acedia* (sloth), vanity, and pride.[5] These vices (and the demons that the monastics as-sociated with them) hinder the Christian and must be addressed by way of ascetical or religious practices such as fasting, access to the sacraments, accountability to others, recourse to helpful counsel, prayer, and immersion in Scripture. The Christian can rest assured that this process is grounded in grace and facilitated by the Spirit, who gently but persistently helps the Christian identify these issues and address them.

The second stage, the illuminative, focuses on growth in knowledge. Patristic theology identifies the two books of God: the *book of Scripture* and the *book of nature*. One's capacity to read these two books and learn from them advances one's knowledge of God and his ways. The book of nature is a metaphor for the observable patterns in the world and the divine "hard-wiring" that informs them. The Church Fathers spoke of the *logoi* (plural of *logos*) in all things, the intentionality that informs, guides, and makes intelligible all things in the world; the *logoi* of creation is its participation in the *Logos* or Reason, which is the Source of all things.[6] The Catholic doctrine of natural law is another instantia-

5. As standardized by Pope Gregory I, the seven deadly sins conflates van-ity and pride into one, partly to make a neat balance with the tradition of the seven gifts of the Spirit derived from Isa 11:1–3.

6. Pope Benedict XVI outlined a Logos theology in a persuasive con-temporary manner in his celebrated "Address to the Regents of Regensburg

tion of reading the book of nature, particularly relevant in an era of such confusion about fundamental matters like sexual differentiation between male and female and the meaning of marriage. Knowledge funds a lifestyle. Ascetical or monastic spirituality places a premium on the contemplation of things from a *katalogical* perspective, that is, from the top down by which the things of this world are illuminated by the truths of its origin, purpose, and destiny.

Finally, there is the unitive way, or way of perfection. Perfection in Christian parlance means a place of completion, of maturity, of approximation toward the goal, and in this stage the Christian moves toward the direct, immediate encounter with God. This is the "pure prayer" as described by figures such as Saint Maximus and associated with the mystical orientation of the saints. This is the mature, seasoned, and suffered spirituality of the "second half" of life, where one's capacity to be aware of and live in the constant presence of God deepens. No one arrives here casually or unscathed, but by way of the first and second steps and all the experiences God in his providence permits one to encounter. The anagogical imagination is both informed by these things and makes sense of them.[7]

Passive *Anagōgē*

The Threefold Way outlines the stages of spiritual development as experienced primarily by those in religious life and communicated in works of ascetical theology. Monastics understood that these stages were a necessary path toward an increasing experience of God's presence and the capacity to indwell life in a conscious awareness of that presence. Throughout Scripture and ascetical literature is the frequent reference to human cooperation with grace,

University." Likewise, Catholic philosopher Peter Kreeft in *The Platonic Tradition*, 50–66. See also Allen "Book of Nature" in *Spiritual Theology*, 109–24.

7. Writers such as Thomas Keating and Richard Rohr are among contemporaries who provides a helpful language for these matters. See Keating, *Crisis of Faith, Crisis of Love*; Rohr, *Falling Upwards*.

of free consent to God's initiatives and the path of ordering one's life according to sacred wisdom.

But in tandem with the active aspects of religious faith—growing in knowledge and consenting to the requirements of each stage—is what can perhaps be simply referred to as the passive dimension of anagogical spirituality, that dimension of development in which one rests in a larger, pervasive work of grace. This "passive" *anagōgē* is generally what is associated with contemplation and the mystical experience (which is adumbrated in the third stage of the Threefold Way, but here is not being considered as something we do as much as that which is done to us).

Something of this is suggested in a passage found in the *Catechism*:

> Contemplation is a *gaze* of faith, fixed on Jesus. "I look at him and he looks at me": this is what a certain peasant of Ars in the time of his holy curé used to say while praying before the tabernacle. This focus on Jesus is a renunciation of self. His gaze purifies our heart; the light of the countenance of Jesus illumines the eyes of our heart and teaches us to see everything in the light of his truth and his compassion for all men. Contemplation also turns its gaze on the mysteries of the life of Christ. Thus it learns the "interior knowledge of our Lord," the more to love him and follow him.[8]

"I look at him and he looks at me." A simple, trusting gaze, apart from efforts and earnestness, stages and strategies. Here again we are reminded of the potential benefits of icons serving in a way like the tabernacle served the contemplative peasant. Here we are invited to simply become increasingly aware of a pervasive divine presence and to live in it and rest in it.[9]

---

8. CCC 2715. The curé of Ars referred to above is Saint John Vianney.

9. There are many devotional publications designed to facilitate this sort of contemplative awareness. See Krill, *Le Point Vierge*.

Conclusion

> Thus anagogy realizes the perfection of both al-
> legory and tropology, achieving their synthesis. . . .
> It integrates the whole and final meaning. It sees, in
> eternity, the fusion of the mystery and the mystic.
> In other words, the eschatological reality attained
> by anagogy is the eternal reality within which every
> other has its consummation. In its final state, it is that
> "new testament, which is the "kingdom of heaven." It
> constitutes "the fullness of Christ."[1]

ONE FINDS IN THEOLOGICAL literature and teaching of the past two centuries not so much as a sustained argument against anagogy as much as sustained neglect. Robert Louis Wilken's recent volume *The Spirit of Early Christian Thought* is a case in point. In a study ranging across the first five centuries of the Christian era, number-ing 321 pages of text besides notes, bibliography, and index, the word anagogy occurs once. This is typical of the literature. But its a good passage and deserves all the attention it can get:

> The term Theodore [of Studium] uses for lifting up the
> mind is *anagogy*, a word that was often used to refer to
> the spiritual sense of the Scriptures. Over time the term
> came to be used to designate future hopes and hence

1. Lubac, *Medieval Exegesis*, 2:187.

to carry eschatological overtones. Theodore seems to understand icons in this sense because he says that in looking at the image one is able to anticipate seeing God face to face, "with one's own eyes." Because the icon is an image of the living Christ, it looks forward as well as back, anticipating the vision of God.[2]

The logic of anagogy, however, hovers over much of Wilken's project, if implicitly so. One chapter is entitled "The End in the Beginning," which opens with an epigraph derived from Gregory of Nyssa, "Since the creation came into being at the beginning through God's power, the end of every thing that exists is inseparably linked to the beginning."[3] The word translated "end" of course does not mean conclusion or cessation, but goal, purpose, reason. Fathers like Gregory reveled in the thought that the end of man— his *raison d'être*—is participation in the divine life, a thought summarized in the concept of *deification*.

The vision and terminology outlined in the passages above are unfamiliar to Catholics in the West because, as has been reviewed above, Western consciousness over the centuries became preoccupied with matters of literalism, naturalism, forensic or legal justification, and delivery from personal guilt. None of these things are bad in of themselves, and much that is laudable has emerged from them. But a reductionism took place in the Western Church, the nadir of which can be summarized as "moralistic, therapeutic deism."

Conditions of a reduced horizon of Christian believing and living has, however, been the subject of redress for some time now, beginning in many ways with Vatican II. As has been suggested, Vatican II gave Catholics renewed permission to engage with Scripture. This has yielded profoundly positive results in terms of lay Catholic formation. Another source of hope has been the retrieval of a thoroughly Trinitarian approach to doctrine and the relational and personalistic understanding this brings both to the subject of theology as well as anthropology and ethics. These

2. Wilken, *Spirit of Early Christian Thought*, 260–61.
3. Wilken, *Spirit of Early Christian Thought*, 136.

61

intellectual and theological movements are both grounded in and draw Christians back towards the resources of the patristic era. Among these resources are the example of life lived immersed in Scripture, worship, prayer, and service, as well as of a certain mind-set this work refers to as an anagogical imagination.[4]

Some reflections along a practical line of thought are probably appropriate at this point.

The anagogical imagination is attuned to the implications of the doctrine of the Trinity, especially in relation to how it presents a Son who assimilates his people into that sonship with him. This is central. All the familiar abstract nouns associated particularly with Saint Paul's description of the Christian experience—salvation, redemption, justification, sanctification, glorification, adoption—are but slices of the feast of assimilation into Christ. There is therefore a body of knowledge of such terms and concepts that needs to be learned, which is usually gained in a process of sustained reading. Besides English language resources, which are noted and recommended in this project, there is an abundance today of freshly translated works of the Church Fathers so frequently referred to in this book. Because of their historical provenance and sometimes unfamiliar terms and concepts, recourse to good introductions are often helpful and a certain patience required of the novice. Saints Athanasius, Gregory of Nyssa, and Maximus the Confessor are among the most recommended for the beginner.

The anagogical imagination is attuned to the trajectory of Scripture and of passages, sometimes explicit and sometimes

---

4. Resources in this regard have been documented throughout this project. Among them are the writings of Benedict XVI (Joseph Cardinal Ratzinger), including the *Catechism of the Catholic Church* (1992, the writing of which was supervised by Cardinal Ratzinger), the text and tenor of which is imbued with the kind of Trinitarian and personalistic emphases endorsed in this book. There are many more such resources and witnesses to these trends. Some of a more scholarly nature include Zizioulas, *Being as Communion*; Boersma, *Heavenly Participation*; and the work of developmental psychologist James Loder, including *The Logic of the Spirit*. Still substantial but more accessible studies include Corbon, *Wellspring of Worship*; Clément, *Roots of Christian Mysticism*; and Maloney, *Abiding in the Indwelling Trinity*. One also notes, with both appreciation and caution, Rohr, *Divine Dance*.

implicit, that point toward a redemption that is both personal and cosmic. Reading Scripture in an anagogical light lends itself to an optimistic orientation towards matters of destiny. God in this perspective is no longer one who grudgingly doles out get-out-of-hell passes. He is perceived rather as accomplishing something of literally cosmic dimensions in and through his Son by his Spirit. Passages such as those cited earlier from Ephesians, Colossians, and Saint John's Gospel, as well as many not directly cited, point toward something many dismiss as too good to be true, especially if raised on a diet of moralistic, therapeutic deism. And in such a reading and immersion in Scripture, one begins to gain a sneaking suspicion that divine love is more encompassing and truly absolving than previously considered.

The anagogical imagination is attuned to the implications of the sacraments. The words of a popular Catholic worship song express patristic theology quite accurately when it speaks of becoming what is received in the Eucharistic feast.[5] Anagogy moves thought away from the transactional toward the transformational. "Here we become what we receive." It moves religious experience away from fast-food, ticket-punching calculations of minimal worship participation toward an understanding that what takes place in worship and sacrament is *real* in the metaphysical sense of the word and therefore worthy of profound attentiveness.

More importantly, during its liturgy, the Christian Church proclaims its *mysterium fidei* ("Christ has died, Christ is risen, Christ will come again!"), it announces a mystery that is in the process of occurring. Scripture, liturgy, word, and sacrament signal and mediate divine actions larger than themselves. Better still, they communicate the Trinitarian initiatives that are still very much in the process of coming to fulfillment. *It is the End that reveals the meaning of the present.* This is anagogy. It is only by remembering and, through grace, imaginatively entering into the future events of Christ's second coming and the glorification

---

5. Chris Muglia, "Our God is Here," (Sound Mission Music, 2001). A sustained and classic exploration of this theme is Schmemann, *For the Life of the World.*

of the cosmos that the final meaning of both Scripture and history is disclosed.

The anagogical imagination becomes attuned to certain themes and episodes in Scripture, some of which have already been considered here. Among these is the ascension of Jesus. Recorded at length in the Gospels of Matthew and Luke and the Book of Acts, it is among the events in the story of Jesus that gets short shrift in the life of the contemporary Church. It is not a subject of depiction in classic iconography, and attempts in the Western pictorial tradition are usually unpersuasive and disappointing. Among the least helpful results of the pictorial representations is to suggest that the ascension represents the departure and subsequent absence of the Lord. The ascension is not about absence but of *a new mode of presence*. This is a difficult matter to convincingly communicate to the faithful in the pew, but it is a necessary and perennial requirement of responsible and transformative ministry. Jean Corbon provides an example of how to synthesize the complexity of the subject in a passage deserving extended quotation:

> In his Ascension, then, Christ did not at all disappear; on the contrary, he began to appear and to come. For this reason, the hymns we use in our churches sing of him as "the Sun of justice" that rises in the east. He who is the splendor of the Father and who once descended into the depths of our darkness is now exalted and fills all things with his light. Our last times are located between that first Ascension and the Ascension that will carry him to the zenith of his glorious parousia. The Lord has not gone away to rest from his redemptive toil; his "work" continues, but now at his Father's side, and because he is there he is now much closer to us, "very near to us," in the work that is the liturgy of the last times. "He leads captives," namely, us, to the new world of his Resurrection and bestows his "gifts," his Spirit, on men. His Ascension is a progressive movement, "from beginning to beginning" [Gregory of Nyssa].
>
> Jesus is, of course, at his Father's side. If, however, we reduce this "ascent" to a particular moment in our mortal history, we simply forget that beginning with the hour of his Cross and Resurrection Jesus and the human

race are henceforth one. He became a son of man in order that we might become sons of God. The Ascension is progressive "until we all . . . form the perfect Man fully mature with the fullness of Christ himself" (Eph 4:13). The movement of Ascension will be complete only when all the members of his body have been drawn to the Father and brought to life by his Spirit. Is this not the meaning of the answer the angels gave to the disciples: "Why are you Galileans standing here looking up into the sky? This Jesus who has been taken up from you into heaven will come back in the same way as you have seen him go into heaven" (Acts 1:11). The Ascension does not show us in advance the setting of the final parousia; it is rather the activation of the Paschal energy of Christ, who "fills all things" (Eph 4:10).[6]

The "activation of the Paschal energy of Christ." This is how one can understand the ascension in a way that moves from a notion of disappearance and absence to one of presence and participation. Corbon relies on the text of Paul's Epistle to the Ephesians, which is a *locus classicus* of the Church's assimilation into Christ's identity and mission.

Another episode that emerges more fully into view is the transfiguration. This of course is a frequent theme depicted in the canon of iconography. A classic hymn of the Oxford Movement of nineteenth-century Anglicanism captures the implications of this episode: "With shining face and bright array / Christ deigns to manifest today / What glory shall be theirs above / Who joy in God with perfect love."[7] The transfiguration is the icon of deification—human nature assimilated to divine grace. The anagogical imagination brings this depiction into the interiority of one's life, allowing it to inform one's growing self-understanding and sense of destiny.

Finally, and perhaps counterintuitively, the anagogical imagination is attuned to the implications of the deposition and burial of Jesus. Here, a former life is concluded and laid to rest. "That

6. Corbon, *Wellspring of Worship*, 61–62.

7. "O Wondrous Type," fifteenth-century Latin hymn, translated by John Mason Neale.

which I was I no longer am" is an anagogical sense of self. Drawing on the believer's union with Christ affected by Baptism, Saint Paul is able to write, "We were buried with him by baptism into death, so that as Christ was raised from the dead by the glory of the Father, we too might walk in newness of life" (Rom 6:4). And: "one thing I do, forgetting what lies behind and straining toward what lies ahead, I press on toward the goal for the prize of the upward call of God in Christ Jesus" (Phil 3:13-14).

* * *

The Church and its eucharistic liturgy are established, in the last analysis, by the *upward call* of Christ the Great High Priest and King. This call is made concrete in the command issued by the priest at the beginning of every Anaphora: "*Sursum corda*! Lift up your hearts!" This cry heralds the miracle of true ecclesial existence: a real participation in the wedding feast of the Lamb—an actual sharing in the heavenly feast, now made mystically present in the divine liturgy on earth in anticipation of its anagogical fullness when Christ comes again. The Eucharist, in other words, is altogether an eschatological and anagogical event. To recall the words of the late Orthodox theologian John Zizioulas, the Church "is what she is by becoming again and again what she will be." She is the bride and body of Christ, formed as a eucharistic assembly, and gathered around the throne of the Lamb who was slain (Rev 5:6, 12). This is a divine assembly, a holy gathering, a priestly people, proclaiming that "Christ has died, Christ is risen, and Christ will come again." The Church lives in hopeful anticipation of its anagogical completion "in Christ." It experiences the upward pull of Christ's ascension, even as it awaits his return in glory. This will occur when God has "put all things under [Christ's] feet and has made him the head over all things for the church, which is his body, the fullness of him who fills all in all" (Eph 1:22-23).

66

Glossary

Anagogy: Derived from Greek meaning "to lead upward," it is one of the four modes of biblical interpretation, along with the literal, the allegorical, and the tropological (or "moral"). The anagogical sense of Scripture is that which illuminates the eschatological as well as the divinizing dimensions of the Christian life. It is a "mystical" dimension of biblical reading in that it illuminates the Christian's present participation in Christ's ascension and heavenly existence.

Analogy: Analogies are acts of reason by which the truth of something is revealed when compared with something else. Classic theology speaks of the *analogia entis*, or the "analogy of being," by which knowledge of God is sought and gained when points of comparison are found between God and creation. On the other hand, the way of the *analogia fidei* emphasizes that truths about God exist in a proportional relation with other revealed truths; truths help explain other truths and so form a coherent relationship with one another.

Anamnesis: Based on the Greek word meaning "remembrance," it is an important term in the Christian celebration of the Eucharist, where the community is commanded to "do this in remembrance of me." Commentators often remark that *anamnesis* is not merely to remember a past event but to recall it in such a way as to experience it. It is the recalling of something that occurred in the past into the lived present. This notion underscores the participatory dynamic of the Christian's relationship with Jesus in his life, death, resurrection, and ascension.

Anaphora: A Greek word meaning "a carrying up," and is the technical term for the prayer of the Eucharist whereby the celebrant "carries up" or lifts before God the sacrifice of the Mass by way of a stylized rehearsal or repetition of God's mighty acts in the history of his people.

Apokatastasis: Greek term meaning "restoration." Etymologically derived from *apo* ("back again"), *kathistemi* ("constitute, set down"), and *stasis*, meaning a state or mode of stability, thus "return to a former state." One thinks of the medical term *homeostasis*, referring to the manner in which the body naturally tends towards a state of health unless otherwise inhibited or injured. The phrase *apokatastaseōs pantōn* occurs in Acts 3:21, where Saint Peter informs his listeners that Jesus "must remain in heaven until the time of the restoration of all things of which God spoke thorough the mouths of the holy prophets." It is this sense of the "restoration of all things" which is picked up and used among certain patristic era theologians in a speculative manner regarding God's eschatological intentions for all creation, including that which was "lost" through the fall.

Ascesis: Greek word meaning "discipline" and associated with athletic training and conditioning. It was adopted into Christian vocabulary as a term associated with spiritual disciplines, such as fasting, habitual prayer, meditation on Scripture, etc.

Ascension (analepsis): The climax of the sequence of events summarized as the Paschal mystery, but arguably of the entire story of the incarnation of the Son of God. Placed in line with his earthly life and his descent into hell, the ascension completes Jesus' entire experience and victory over every element of human existence. The ascension marks Jesus' victory over the "prince of the power of the air" (Eph 2:2) and of his enthronement at the Father's right hand, from where he sends his Spirit and intercedes for his people. The ascension of Jesus is anticipated in such Old Testament episodes as the "assumptions" of Enoch (Gen 5:25; Heb 11:5), Elijah (2 Kgs 2:11), and later of the Blessed Virgin.

Aseity: A technical term describing God's transcendence, God's completeness-in-himself, so that all his acts and relations towards his people are based in grace, not necessity.

Cappadocians: The Cappadocians, or the Cappadocian Fathers, refer to Sts. Basil of Caesarea, Gregory of Nyssa (Basil's brother), and their colleague Gregory of Nazianzus, theologians of the fourth century. These three bishops played a significant role in developing the way the Church understands and articulates the nature of personhood and how this is perceived in the Trinity, in the incarnation of the Son, and in the transformation of humanity.

Chalcedonian Definition: The Council of Chalcedon was held in 451 in what is now Turkey. Refuting the teachings of Eutychus and Nestorius, the Council gave definitive articulation of Jesus' existence as one person in two natures—divine and human. This definition provides the Church with an important resource for understanding how the divine and the human do not collapse into each other but constitute the integrated consciousness within the person of Jesus. The definition likewise provides insight into how relationality exists—non-competitive coherence—among the persons of the Trinity, between God and his Son incarnate, in the association of Jesus and the Church, and within healthy, non-competitive human interactions.

Communio Personarum: Latin for "communion of persons," it refers to the dynamic of relationality revealed within God's own Triune existence and as the ideal dynamic of human well-being—person-in-relationship-with-others—restored by the Spirit through Jesus.

Connaturality: "It takes one to know one." This saying captures the notion communicated in the term "connatural," the idea that by way of a process of transformation, two previously unlike things take on a recognizable and participatory similarity. Moral theologians speak of how divine qualities become connatural to the Christian through the process of formation. Mystics emphasize how the Holy Spirit and human spirit increasingly share a connatural relationship in the process of deification.

Corpus Tri-forme: An interpretation of Jesus' trans-temporal modes of existence. Corpus Tri-forme refers to Jesus' existence as (1) the historical Jesus, (2) the Eucharistic victim, and (3) the ecclesial body. This interpretation of Jesus' existence allows for a greater perception that Jesus is never merely the historical figure now assumed into heaven, but a relational-dynamic person whose fullness (*pleroma*) includes all those incorporated into his reality.

Cosmos: The Greek term *kosmos* is often used interchangeably with the word "universe." In Greek natural philosophy, the term meant the "orderly arrangement" of all things, the beautiful functioning of all that is seen (thus the term "cosmetics"). *Kosmos* is the word used most often in the Greek Scriptures for "world."

Deification/Divinization (see Theosis)

Economy: The English word is derived from Greek *oikonomia* (*economia*) and has several has meanings in theological usage. Primarily it means an administration or stewardship over something. It can also mean "dispensation" or "ordered plan," as Saint Paul uses it for example in Eph 3:9 when he writes of "the plan (*oikonomia*) of the mystery hidden for ages in God." In later theology, "economy" is used to refer to the outer workings of God in salvation, in contrast to theology, which properly speaking involves the revelation of the inner life of God. The *Catechism* summarizes this in the following manner:

> The Fathers of the Church distinguish between theology (*theologia*) and economy (*oikonomia*). "Theology"

refers to the mystery of God's inmost life within the Blessed Trinity and "economy" to all the works by which God reveals himself and communicates his life. Through the *oikonomia* the *theologia* is revealed to us; but conversely, the *theologia* illuminates the whole *oikonomia*. God's works reveal who he is in himself; the mystery of his inmost being enlightens our understanding of all his works. So it is, analogously, among human persons. A person discloses himself in his actions, and the better we know a person, the better we understand his actions. (CCC 236)

Eros: One of several words from Greek translated in English as "love." Originally the name of a god of sexual attraction (Cupid in its Latin form), the word came to be used in natural philosophy as an assimilating, unifying force of attraction in the world. The word is not used in the New Testament for love (*agape* is the most frequently occurring, followed by *philia*). Recent Catholic theology has sought to rehabilitate the term in order to (1) further validate sexuality as a dimension of human personhood, (2) to describe the natural desire for God implanted in the human soul, and (3) to illuminate the relationality within the Trinity often described as *perichoresis*. Pope Benedict XVI explored these themes in his encyclical *Deus Caritas Est* ("God Is Love").

Eschatology: Technical term for the "study of last things," and as such is associated with the themes of heaven, hell, death, and judgment. More broadly, eschatology encompasses the biblical understanding of time, of the meaning of history, and the drive from creation to the kingdom of God. The "eschatological tension" between the "now" (the present if imperfect manifestation of the kingdom in the Church and her ministries) and the "not yet" (its full revelation to the world-at-large) is a central feature of Christian living.

Ekstasis: Greek word referring the experience of being "outside oneself" and the source of the English term "ecstasy." Common usage today tends to associate ecstasy with exuberant happiness or joy, but the term refers to any experience that draws a person outside themselves. The term is employed to describe the relational out-going of each person of the Trinity toward the other and likewise the transcendental experience of a Christian growing in their awareness of their incorporation in the Son and all the good that this includes.

Historical-Critical Method: A term of art referring to the study of texts in which initial or even entire meaning is sought in relation to matters of originating context, language, and authorship. It is related primarily to the literal level of Scriptural interpretation and, as such, is recognized as having provided necessary and helpful illuminations of the biblical text. Pope Benedict XVI was particularly insightful in identifying both the helpful contributions and the inherent limitations of historical-critical methodologies in biblical research.

Hypostasis: Very important technical term in Trinitarian theology. Functionally in Christian theology *hypostasis* means "person," and so is used to speak of the persons of the Father, Son, and Holy Spirit co-inhering as one God. *Hypostasis* applied to Jesus describes his existence as one person in two natures—divine and human, or the "hypostatic union" as it is frequently referred to. The word is often juxtaposed with another important Trinitarian term, *ousia,* functionally defined as "substance." Both terms have complicated etymological background stories, and both are important in understanding God and experiencing God's presence.

Icons: The word icon is derived from the Greek *eikōn* and means "image." The word occurs in Col 1:15 and 2 Cor 4:4, for example, to describe Christ as a the "image" of God. Icons are religious paintings, generally executed on wood panels. Icons retain a privileged place in Christian liturgy and life for the manner in which they serve as "visual theology." *Iconography* literally means "icon writing," because the icon is seen as functioning much like the words of Scripture—a medium of the human environment (words, texts, images, etc.) through which the divine and human can meet and communicate.

Immanence: Theological term describing God's "nearness," God's presence within and towards the created realm. It is usually set in contrast to "transcendence," which is used to describe God's set-apartness from the created realm, God's otherness, the religious analog to the concept of "holiness."

Katalogical: From the Greek word for "category," the term is used to describe knowledge of God derived from special revelation, as distinct from knowledge of God derived from analogical reasoning. Katalogical (or categorical) reasoning is described as coming "from the top down," while analogical reasoning is described as coming "from the bottom up." Both movements are necessary in a wholistic and comprehensive knowledge and experience of God.

Kenosis: Greek word used by Saint Paul to describe the "self-emptying" of the Son of God in his incarnation (Phil 2:7). Such "self-emptying" or self-donation is perceived as the reciprocal regard the persons of the Trinity pay to each other. It can also be seen in the Spirit's self-emptying presence in Christ's body and becomes a chief aspect of the basic Christian posture toward others.

Kerygma: Greek word meaning message or announcement. It is used in the New Testament to refer to the act of preaching, and in time was used to refer to the *preached message about salvation.*

Koinonia: Greek word for "fellowship," suggestive of participation with someone in something. It is an important term in contemplative spirituality as it describes the basic dynamic of a relationship with God.

Lectio Divina: From Latin for "divine or religious reading." It is a practice of reading Scripture derived from the monastic tradition which has been revived and embraced particularly among lay Christians since the latter quarter of the twentieth century. Often practiced in group settings, it is a method of Bible reading that places an emphasis on encounter with God in and through the text. Often combined with dynamics of open conversation, contemplative reflection, and prayerful response to the passage at hand.

Leitourgia: Greek word referring to "a public work" and adopted by the Christian community to indicate their corporate worship of God. It is the source of the term "liturgy." The word can also be used to describe the entire life of the Christian in their continual and ever-deepening public life of praise toward the Father.

Logos: Greek term with a wide range of meaning. The root of the English term "logic" and of the suffix indicating categories of knowledge and study (bio*logy*, socio*logy*, etc.), *logos* was employed in the ancient world to describe the source of the rationality of things, as well as the unspoken intentionality behind an act that explains the reason why an act was undertaken. It is in this sense that Saint John famously uses the term in the opening of his gospel account to portray Jesus as the "Word" (*Logos*) of God who is the agent of all of God's creative and redemptive purposes. An important strand of early Church theology, often referred to as "Logos theology," exists in which theologians sought to identify Christ's presence in all forms of knowledge and human endeavor.

Midrash: Hebrew term meaning "interpretation" as applied to the Bible. Rabbinic midrash operated on the principle that Scripture consisted of both a literal level of meaning (*peshat*) and a contemporary application of Scripture (*darash*). Rabbis deployed several different techniques in order to tease out the significance of a text or of a theme in Scripture. Saints Matthew and Paul reflect these techniques in a particular way in the text of the New Testament.

Monarchia: Greek word from which "monarchy" is derived, it is used, especially in the Eastern Church, to describe God the Father as the source of the Trinity and the goal toward which the ministries of the Son and the Spirit are intended. The Father *begets* the Son, and the Spirit *proceeds* from their spontaneous love. Generational and procedural terminology, however, should never obscure the fundamental simultaneity of the relationship of the Three Persons with the Trinity.

Mystagogy: Greek term meaning "leading towards or training in mystery," and generally used in reference to the teaching of catechumens in preparation for the reception of baptism and Eucharist. "Mysteries" is the older and still used term for the sacraments. In a larger sense, mystagogy is any leading towards or training in mystery, including the truths and experience of the gospel in general.

Mystery: A frequently used word in the Christian lexicon, a mystery is some aspect of reality not immediately accessible to casual consideration but something that becomes more apparent and clear in light of divine disclosure, personal attentiveness, and lingering contemplation. The English word "mystery" is derived from the Greek *mysterion* and is sometimes translated as "secret," which aptly captures something of the dynamic of mystery. The word *mystery* today is most often associated with the sacraments in contemporary liturgical practice. Certain strands of twentieth-century philosophical reflection, particularly associated with phenomenology, emphasized that mystery identifies some aspect of reality that requires personal participation in order for its truth or reality to become accessible and meaningful.

Mysticism: A dimension of spirituality associated with contemplation and the grace of personal encounter with the divine. Mystics are those engaged in the practices of Christian spirituality (*ascesis*) and who in the midst of their disciplined lives increasingly experience the direct and unmediated presence of God. Literature of the past was usually differentiated between the ascetical and the mystical, but today both are typically joined together under the heading of spirituality or spiritual theology.

Ontology: The study of the modes of existing things, of the nature of *being* and of the being or existence of particular things. To inquire into the ontological status of a given subject, one is asking how "real" something is and how that reality is expressed and encountered. A related term is metaphysics. Metaphysics addresses what is perceived to ground all physics, that is, all movement and existence. As such, metaphysics is generally perceived as a philosophical rather than a scientific enterprise since often it is asking questions beyond the reach of ordinary scientific analysis. For Aristotle, metaphysics was the "first philosophy" because it addresses matters of fundamental, primary concern. Christian theology situates metaphysical questions in terms of its doctrines of God and creation.

Ousia: See *Hypostasis.*

Parousia: Greek term meaning "nearness," of being alongside of someone, but used to refer to the presence of Christ and his manifestation at the end of time, that is, his coming again "to judge the living and the dead."

Participation: The concept of participation is communicated in the New Testament in the Greek words *koinonia*, generally translated as "fellowship," and *methexis*, translated as a sharing in something. To participate in or with somebody or something is to have some form of fellowship with it, a shared experience, or some form of resemblance or similarity. There is a rich philosophical heritage associated with the concept of participation, especially in Platonic philosophy in relation to the question of how smaller units share in the identity of a larger or originating source—how the part shares in the whole. That humans can share or participate in one another's existence and in the divine life is a matter central to the New Testament.

Patristic Theology: Derived from the Greek word for "father," patristic theology, the study of which is often referred to as patristics, is concerned with the teachings of key figures (or Church Fathers, typically but not always bishops) across the first eight centuries of the Christian era. Patristic theology is associated with the great doctrinal affirmations and anathemas canonized in the first seven ecumenical councils (Nicea I, Constantinople I, Ephesus I and II, Chalcedon, Constantinople II, and Nicea II). An important element in patristic theology is the contribution of the monastic experience. Much of the spiritual theology derived from patristic sources (in both ascetical and mystical emphases) is of monastic origin.

Perichoresis: Greek word meaning "interaction" or "rotation," from *perichōreō*, and adopted in Christian theology to describe the interpenetrating movement or presence of the persons of the Trinity within each other The word is useful in giving articulation to the mutually-indwelling character of relations within the Trinity, which can in turn provide insight into the mutual-indwelling character of the relation between Jesus and his people; see John 14:11, 20, 23.

Person: An instantiation of being with the powers of intentionality, affection, reason, and communicative presence. In light of Trinitarian theology, a person is fundamentally a being capable of *relationship.* In Catholic anthropology and ethics, "person" stands for a human in their existence as an image of God and inalienable from that status from conception through natural death. The concept of personhood is an important element in Catholic theology and social doctrine. It was the work of the Cappadocian Fathers who provided the Church with resources to conceptualize what constitutes a person, both divine and human. The declaration *Dignitas Infinita* (April 8, 2024) provides a renewed emphasis on this dimension of the Catholic doctrine of human existence. The role of the body is also an integral aspect of the Catholic analysis of personhood (see CCC 362–65).

"Person-Relation" Ontology: A major theme in recent Trinitarian theology that aims to redress an imbalance within theologies of God that tend to emphasize a shared divine "stuff" (a "substance ontology") rather than or prior to an irreducible divine existence as persons.

Pleroma: Greek word meaning "fullness." Used casually in the New Testament to refer to the completion or filling up of something (see Matt 13:48), and more technically by Saint Paul, especially in the Epistles to the Ephesians and Colossians. In these documents, *pleroma* is used to describe the "fullness" of deity that dwelt bodily in Jesus (Col 1:19), the spiritual fullness available to Christians in union with Jesus (Col 2:9–10; Eph 3:19), and the fullness of the body of Christ when incorporating all who belong to him (Eph 1:22–23). The word *pleroma* may have been a buzzword among dissidents later referred to as "gnostics" in their claims to a "fuller" knowledge of Christ than that available in the apostolic Church. Saint Paul's adoption of the word is then seen as an implicit critique of such claims.

Prolepsis: A technical but useful word to describe the future-oriented character of Christian identity. It is a term found within the constellation of terms associated with *eschatology*. Derived from Greek, the word basically means "anticipation." Christians live their lives *proleptically* in the sense that they no longer define themselves exclusively in terms of who they used to be or even what they appear to be in the present, but what they will be when the Son of God is disclosed at the end of time. The classic biblical expression of this dynamic is 1 John 3:2–3, "Beloved, we are God's children *now*; it does *not yet* appear what we shall be, but we know that when he appears we shall be like him, for we shall see him as he is." To live in the confidence that this passage expresses is to live proleptically, and in this sense the term is part of what is advanced in the present project as an anagogical imagination.

Prosopon: From the Greek meaning "face" or "mask" as used in the ancient theater, it was adopted in Christian theology as another way of speaking of a *person*. The word emphasizes the personal character of the divine persons by highlighting the face as that feature which we so commonly associated with the presence of a person. Saint Paul speaks of God's glory revealed in the face of Jesus (2 Cor 4:6), and the great hope of biblical saints is to see the face of God.

Protology: From Greek, the study of first things. In Christian theology, such first things focus primarily on matters related to the purpose and process of creation. In the present study it is argued that the first things are illuminated in light of the last things; eschatology illuminates protology.

Realized Eschatology: This phrase refers to the ways in which God's final intentions for all things in salvation are perceived and experienced in the present and are operating now in the world. God's final intention for all things is summarized biblically in the concept of the kingdom of God, and so realized eschatology generally represents doctrinal reflection on the manifestation of God's kingdom in the present within the Church and its ministries.

Recapitulation: Latin-derived word not found in the New Testament but useful as another way of highlighting the unity of the Old and New Testaments. Dynamics of recapitulation are perceived, for example, in the way in which aspects of the Old Testament, particularly the history of Israel, is revisited, relived, and redeemed in the life of Jesus. On a broader scale, it is perceived that in Jesus the whole of human existence is revisited, relived, and redeemed, further confirming Jesus as the Head (Latin *capitalis* "of the head") of the Church and of the entire cosmos.

Ressourcement: A French term describing a "return to sources," namely those of the patristic age which animated the rise, as first used by its critics, of a *nouvelle théologie* ("new theology"), especially but not exclusively among French-speaking Catholic theologians in the middle years of the twentieth century. Sometimes perceived as working in tandem with and sometimes perceived as competing with Thomistic theology (often referred to as neo-scholasticism) as sources of Catholic theological and liturgical renewal. Both movements played significant roles in the formation of the documents that emerged from the Second Vatican Council (1962–65).

Sacrament: An efficacious *sign* that contains, embodies, conveys, communicates, and manifests the invisible mystery to which it points. Sacraments are said to transcend mere symbols by the fact that sacraments directly participate in the reality with which they are associated and therefore can effectively communicate or conduct divine presence and grace. As such, sacraments are mysteries that initiate and increasingly conform participants to the mystery that is the gospel experience.

Salvation History: A term of art in biblical studies that describes the manner in which God reveals himself and his purposes to his people over time. Essentially, salvation history is the content of Scripture from the Old to the New Testaments. "The whole history of salvation is identical with the history of the way and the means by which the one true God, Father, Son and Holy Spirit, reveals himself to men 'and reconciles and unites with himself those who turn away from sin'" (CCC 234).

Senses of Scripture: "According to an ancient tradition, one can distinguish between two *senses* of Scripture: the literal and the spiritual, the latter being subdivided into the allegorical, moral, and anagogical senses. The profound concordance of the four senses guarantees all its richness to the living reading of Scripture in the Church" (CCC 115). By "senses" the Church means that Scripture addresses its receivers in a multivalent manner. The Church has long recognized the literal sense, that is, the meaning conveyed at its most literary and historical level, as the foundation of biblical interpretation. The spiritual sense of Scripture emerges from attentive, contemplative immersion in the text where it yields "deeper" meanings that correspond with the literal level but also transcend it. This project focuses on the level that "leads upwards," that is, speaks to the ascended identity of the Church and its members, a meaning taken from literal readings of the text but derived from an "analogy of faith" by which various strands of biblical and Church teaching are brought together collaborative effect.

***Telos* (teleology):** Greek word meaning the "goal" or "end" toward which something aims. The biblical worldview is said to be *teleological* because it moves from a definitive beginning toward a definitive goal—the kingdom of God. Teleology is the study of the ends or purposes of things.

Theandric: An adjective derived from the Greek words *theos* ("divine") and *andros* ("human"), combined to create a term describing (1) divine action through a created or human medium and (2) joint action of divine and human intentionality.

Theophany: A visible appearance of the divine to human consciousness. Several theophanies are reported in the Old Testament, including the visitation to Abraham, the angel who wrestled with Jacob, and the burning bush. To describe an event as *theophanic* is to mean that in some event or encounter divine presence or purpose is disclosed or made accessible, usually in some visual form and in a communicative manner, to human reception. A related term is *epiphany*, meaning an appearance or manifestation of some sort, often of a divine kind.

Theosis/Theopoeia: Greek terms used to express the deification or divinization of human existence. To be deified or divinized is to be so penetrated with the divine through active faith and sacramental participation in the Church as to grow in connaturality with the divine and so enjoy fellowship with God's nature. A classic passage is 2 Pet 1:3–4. While always remaining human, salvation introduces a process of transformation that patristic theologians describe in a variety of ways, deification being chief among them. *Theosis* or deification refers to that transformation and transfiguration by which Christians come to not merely imitate Jesus but to actually share in his divine quality of life. This transformation is given visual expression in icons of saints.

Totus Christus: Latin phrase meaning the "whole Christ," and generally used in reference to the relationship between the Son of God and his body, the Church, which together, bound in spiritual unity, sacramental presence, and ordained ministry constitute the whole Christ. Rooted in the Trinitarian perception that even the divine persons are complete only in relation with each other (see *perichoresis*), the doctrine of *Totus Christus* maintains that Jesus is complete only in relationship with his body, the people he has won to himself.

Transcendence: Derived from Latin meaning to rise out of or above other things, the term is used in theology to describe God's "otherness" from the created realm, the metaphysical analogue to God's holiness. Christian theology has always maintained, with some difficulty, the dialectic between God's transcendence and God's immanence, of his being "beyond" and his being "near" to the created realm. A classic passage that expresses this dual reality is Isa 57:15 ("I dwell in the high and holy place, and also with him who is of a contrite and humble spirit").

Transfiguration: An important episode in the life of Jesus that the Synoptic Gospels portray as inaugurating the fateful journey to Jerusalem. In this sense it plays a parallel function with the baptism at the beginning of Jesus public ministry, both of which include the Father's voice affirming the Son's identity and a visual sign of divine presence preceding the beginning of significant undertakings. The transfiguration bears similarity with other *theophanies* or visual manifestations of divine presence which occur in the Old Testament (i.e. the burning bush). At the transfiguration the apostles saw the divinity that permeated the humanity of the Son of God, a permeation not unlike that which accompanies deification.

Trinity: "The mystery of the Most Holy Trinity is the central mystery of Christian life and faith" (CCC 234). The English word Trinity is derived from the Greek *trias* and the Latin *trinitas* and aims at identifying the complex unity and interpenetrating relationality that constitutes the existence of God as Father, Son, and Holy Spirit.

***Tropos* (tropology):** From Greek, meaning "the way in which" or the "manner with which one thing is related to (or oriented towards) another." In literature a *trope* is a conventional form or stylized manner of expressing something. In Catholic biblical interpretation, the tropological sense of Scripture refers to its moral dimension, what a passage means in relation to the moral life.

Typology: A very important dimension of biblical interpretation. Typology seeks to relate figures, patterns, and events from the Old Testament to their corresponding figures, patterns, and events in the New Testament. The basic idea is that a *type* from the Old is fulfilled in it's *antitype* in the New. Early Christian and patristic exegetes sought to find Christ in the Old Testament, and they did so by way of locating correspondences between the Testaments. Saint Paul established and validated the practice in his own typological interpretation of Sarah and Hagar (Gal 4:21–31; see also Rom 5:14); the method is found throughout the Letter to the Hebrews. Typology is a crucial dimension of any *spiritual* (allegorical, tropological, or anagogical) appropriation of the Bible as it illuminates the presence of Jesus and the continuity of God's purposes throughout the Old and New Testaments as well as identifying the believer's own mystical participation in the personal existence and ministry of the Son of God.

Recommended Reading

Patristic Theology and Biblical Interpretation

Allen, Diogenes. *Spiritual Theology: The Theology of Yesterday for Spiritual Help Today*. Boston: Cowley, 1997. The theology of "yesterday" in the subtitle is patristic theology, and this is an excellent and thoroughly accessible introduction to this subject matter. The practical implications of this theology is central to Allen's project. Highly recommended.

Athanasius. *On the Incarnation*. Translated by John Behr. New York: Saint Vladimir's Seminary Press, 2011. This edition of Athanasius' celebrated treatise is available in the Saint Vladimir's Seminary Popular Patristics Series, which makes available many valuable texts in patristic theology. Excellent translations in generally inexpensive formats and accompanied with helpful introductions, the series is a recommended source for patristic study. This particular text is central and foundational for all patristic doctrine and is necessary reading for any serious student.

Augustine. *On Christian Teaching (De Doctrina Christiana)*. Translated by R. P. H. Green. Oxford: Oxford University Press, 1997. A foundational treatise on the exegesis of Scripture written by the great North African bishop early in his career. In some ways a better text with which to begin a study of Augustine than the *Confessions* as it is briefer and less given to speculative matters. Saint Augustine largely set the terms of all subsequent Western Church theology.

Gregory of Nazianzus. *The Five Theological Orations and Two Letters to Cledonius.* Translated by Frederick Williams and Lionel Wickham. New York: Saint Vladimir's Seminary Press, 2002. "Discussion of theology is not for everyone, I tell you, not for everyone—it is no such inexpensive or effortless pursuit" (Oration 27.3). Doubtless true. But this volume includes that great patristic maxim of incarnation theology: "The unassumed is the unhealed, but what is united with God is being saved." The Five Orations are essential and enduring texts in Christian doctrine.

Gregory of Nyssa. *The Life of Moses.* Translated by Abraham J. Malherbe and Everett Ferguson. Mahwah, NJ: Paulist, 1978. Part of the Paulist Press Classics of Western Spirituality series, this is an excellent edition of this significant text. One of the celebrated Cappadocian Fathers, Gregory of Nyssa's work has received a revived interest among both scholars and interested laypeople. This text is a classic of patristic biblical interpretation and introduces its readers both to contours of such interpretation as well as to important points of Gregory's distinct theological convictions.

Maximus the Confessor. *Selected Writings.* Translated by George C. Berthold. Mahwah, NJ: Paulist, 1985. While all five texts included in this translation are commended, particular attention is being drawn to "The Four Hundred Chapters on Love" and "The Church's Mystagogy." The first is a classic of ascetical theology, that is, of spiritual practice toward full experiential union with God. The latter is a classic of the mystagogical tradition.

Icons

Baggley, John. *Doors of Perception: Icons and their Spiritual Significance.* New York: Saint Vladimir's Seminary Press, 1988. Currently out of print but still able to be found, this is a wonderful introduction to icons for the uninitiated. The text explores the origins of icons, the principles of their production, the classic themes in the canon, and includes wonderful color plates of important examples.

Beckett, Wendy. *Real Presence: In Search of the Earliest Icons.* New York: Continuum, 2010. Brief, warmly composed, and profusely illustrated with beautiful examples, follow a Catholic art critic as she encounters icons from the foundation of the tradition.

General Resources

Benedict XVI, Pope. *The Word of the Lord (Verbum Domini).* Boston: Pauline, 2010. The work and magisterium of Pope Benedict (Joseph Ratzinger) hovers over this project in a pervasive manner. Anything by Ratzinger/ Benedict is commended to the reader, but this particular text provides a brief but complete statement of his approach to biblical interpretation and its role in spiritual formation.

Boersma, Hans. *Embodiment and Virtue in Gregory of Nyssa: An Anagogical Approach.* Oxford: Oxford University Press, 2013. An excellent study of the theology of Gregory in relation to matters of "bodies": textual, gendered, ecclesial, etc. Boersma situates anagogy as central to Gregory's whole program. Sophisticated scholarship but worth the effort.

———. *Heavenly Participation: The Weaving of a Sacramental Tapestry.* Grand Rapids: Eerdmans, 2011. A popularized edition of a longer scholarly monograph, Boersma roots his project squarely in the line of the *ressourcement* movement. An excellent introduction to the *nouvelle théologie* and its contribution to the recovery of a more participatory and sacramental understanding of the knowledge of God and of the Christian experience.

Catechism of the Catholic Church. Translated by the United States Catholic Conference, Inc. New York: Doubleday, 1995. There simply is no better and more comprehensive summary of Catholic doctrine in one volume. Excellent for both the newcomer and seasoned communicant. The fourth section on Christian Prayer is particularly related to this project, and a slow, meditative reading of it is highly recommended.

Corbon, Jean. *The Wellspring of Worship.* San Francisco: Ignatius, 2005. Highly recommended. Corbon served in the Eastern Melkite Church and was the major contributor to the fourth section of the *Catechism* on Christian Prayer. A book to be savored slowly.

Clément, Olivier. *The Roots of Christian Mysticism.* 2nd ed. New York: New City, 1993. An expansive but accessible introduction to the theology of "yesterday" with a firm eye toward contemporary application. Written by a French Orthodox theologian, this text is a whirlwind tour of the key names and themes in patristic theology. Brief biographical and thematic essays provide a very helpful orientation to the Church of the first eight centuries.

Keating, Thomas. *The Better Part: Stages of Contemplative Living.* New York: Continuum, 2000. Fr. Keating was a monk of the Cistercian Order and generally identified with the movement of Centering Prayer which he developed and promoted in his writings and lectures. This brief book is a gem of monastic theology and psychology, written for the layperson. The opening analysis of the "spiritual sense" of the famous Mary and Martha passage form Luke 11 is a great introduction to the manner in which the Church Fathers engaged with the biblical text and understood progress in the Christian life.

Krill, Philip, and James McCullough. *Life in the Trinity: The Mystery of God and Human Deification.* Eugene, OR: Wipf & Stock, 2022. Explores the implications of the doctrine of the Trinity and especially of the Chalcedonian Definition in order to ground and promote a "mystic" spirituality in the present day. In many ways a companion volume to the present project.

Bibliography

Alison, James. *Raising Abel: The Recovery of an Eschatological Imagination.* New York: Crossroads, 2000.

Allen, Diogenes. *The Path of Perfect Love.* Rev. ed. Boston: Cowley, 1992.

———. *Philosophy for Understanding Theology.* 2nd ed. Louisville: Westminster John Knox, 2007.

———. *Spiritual Theology: The Theology of Yesterday for Spiritual Help Today.* Boston: Cowley, 1997.

Aquinas, Thomas. *Summa Theologica.* https://www.thelatinlibrary.com/aquinas/summa.shtml.

Athanasius. *On the Incarnation.* Translated by John Behr. Crestwood, NY: St. Vladimir's Seminary Press, 2011.

Augustine. *On Christian Teaching.* Translated by R. H. P. Green. Oxford: Oxford University Press, 1997.

Baggley, John. *Doors of Perception: Icons and Their Spiritual Significance.* New York: St. Vladimir's Seminary Press, 1988.

Balthasar, Hans Urs von. *The Glory of the Lord: A Theological Aesthetics, I: Seeing the Form.* San Francisco: Ignatius, 1982.

———. *Theo-Drama: Theological Dramatic Theory I: Prolegomena.* San Francisco: Ignatius, 1988.

———. *Theo-Drama: Theological Dramatic Theory IV: The Action.* San Francisco: Ignatius, 1994.

———. *Theo-Drama: Theological Dramatic Theory V: The Last Act.* San Francisco: Ignatius, 1998.

———. *Theo-Logic—Theological Logical Theory II: Truth of God.* Translated by Aidan J. Walker. San Francisco: Ignatius, 2004.

Barron, Robert. *The Priority of Christ: Towards a Postliberal Catholicism.* Grand Rapids: Brazos, 2007.

Beckett, Wendy. *Real Presence: In Search of the Earliest Icons.* New York: Continuum, 2010.

Behr, John. *The Mystery of Christ: Life in Death.* Crestwood, NY: St. Vladimir's Seminary Press, 2006.

Benedict XVI, Pope. "Address to the Regents of Regensburg University." https://www.vatican.va/content/benedict-xvi/en/speeches/2006/september/documents/hf_ben-xvi_spe_20060912_university-regensburg.html.

———. *Credo for Today: What Christian Believe.* San Francisco: Ignatius, 2009.

———. *Deus Caritas Est (God Is Love).* Boston: Pauline, 2006.

———. *Dogma and Preaching: Applying Christian Doctrine to Daily Life.* Translated Michael J. Miller and Michael J. O'Connell. San Francisco: Ignatius, 2009.

———. *The Feast of Faith: Approaches to a Theology of the Liturgy.* Translated Graham Harrison. San Francisco: Ignatius, 1986.

———. "Homily for Msgr. Luigi Giusanni." *Communio* 31 (2004) 685–87.

———. *Jesus of Nazareth: From the Baptism in the Jordan to the Transfiguration.* Translated by Adrian J. Walker. San Francisco: Ignatius, 2007.

———. *Jesus of Nazareth: Holy Week—From the Entrance into Jerusalem to the Resurrection.* Translated by Vatican Secretariat of State. San Francisco: Ignatius, 2011.

———. *Jesus of Nazareth: The Infancy Narratives.* Translated by Philip J. Whitmore. San Francisco: Ignatius, 2012.

———. *Principles of Catholic Theology: Building Stones for a Fundamental Theology.* Translated R. Mary Frances McCarthy. San Francisco: Ignatius, 1987.

———. *Sacramentum Caritatis (The Sacrament of Charity).* Vatican City: Libreria Editrice Vaticana, 2007.

———. *Spe Salvi (Saved in Hope).* Boston: Pauline, 2007.

———. *Verbum Domini (The Word of the Lord).* Boston: Pauline, 2010.

Bobrinskoy, Boris. *The Mystery of the Trinity: Trinitarian Experience and Vision in the Biblical and Patristic Tradition.* Crestwood, NY: St. Vladimir's Seminary Press, 1999.

Boersma, Hans. *Embodiment and Virtue in Gregory of Nyssa: An Anagogical Approach.* Oxford: Oxford University Press, 2013.

———. *Heavenly Participation: The Weaving of a Sacramental Tapestry.* Grand Rapids: Eerdmans, 2011.

Bray, Gerald. *Biblical Interpretation: Past and Present.* Downers Grove, IL: InterVarsity, 1996.

Brown, David. *God and Enchantment of Place: Reclaiming Human Experience.* Oxford: Oxford University Press, 2004.

———. *God and Grace of Body: Sacrament in Ordinary.* Oxford: Oxford University Press, 2007.

Cameron, John Peter. *Benedictus: Day by Day with Pope Benedict XVI.* San Francisco: Ignatius, 2006.

Catechism of the Catholic Church. Translated by the United States Catholic Conference, Inc. New York: Doubleday, 1995.

Christensen, Michael J., and Jeffrey Wittung. *Partakers of the Divine Nature: The History and Development of Deification in the Christian Traditions.* Grand Rapids: Baker Academic, 2007.

Clément, Olivier. *On Being Human: A Spiritual Anthropology.* New York: New City, 2000.

———. *The Roots of Christian Mysticism: Texts from the Patristic Era with Commentary.* Hyde Park, NY: New City, 1993.

Corbon, Jean. *The Wellspring of Worship.* San Francisco: Ignatius, 2005.

Covey, Stephen R. *The Seven Habits of Highly Effective People.* New York: Free, 1989.

Crosby, John. *Personalist Papers.* Washington, DC: The Catholic University of America Press, 2004.

———. *The Selfhood of the Human Person.* Washington, DC: The Catholic University of America Press, 1966.

Cunningham, David S. *These Three Are One: The Practice of Trinitarian Theology.* Oxford: Blackwell, 1998.

Cunningham, Lawrence S., and Keith J. Egan. *Christian Spirituality: Themes from the Tradition.* Mahwah, NJ: Paulist, 1996.

Daley, Brian E. *God Visible: Patristic Christology Reconsidered.* Oxford: Oxford University Press, 2018.

———. "The *Nouvelle Théologie* and the Patristic Revival: Sources, Symbols, and the Science of Theology." *International Journal of Systematic Theology* 7 (2005) 362–82.

Dickens, W. T. *Hans Urs von Balthasar's Theological Aesthetics: A Model for Post-Critical Biblical Interpretation.* Notre Dame: University of Notre Dame Press, 2003.

Dubay, Thomas. *. . . And You Are Christ's: The Charism of Virginity and the Celibate Life.* San Francisco: Ignatius, 1987.

———. *Fire Within: St. Teresa of Avila, St. John of the Cross, and the Gospel— On Prayer.* San Francisco: Ignatius, 1989.

Edwards, L. Clifton. *Creation's Beauty as Revelation: Toward a Creational Theology of Natural Beauty.* Eugene, OR: Pickwick, 2014.

Evagrios the Solitary (Evagrius Ponticus). "On Prayer." In *The Philokalia, Volume 1,* edited by G. E. H. Palmer et al., 55–71. London: Faber & Faber, 1979.

———. *The Praktikos and Chapters on Prayer.* Translated by John E. Bamberger. Kalamazoo, MI: Cistercian, 1972.

Fagerberg, David. *Consecrating the World: On Mundane Theology.* Kettering, OH: Angelico, 2016.

———. *On Liturgical Asceticism.* Washington, DC: The Catholic University of America Press, 2013.

———. *Theologia Prima: What Is Liturgical Theology?* Chicago: Hillenbrand, 2004.

Farrow, Douglas. *Ascension and Ecclesia: On the Significance of the Ascension for Ecclesiology and Christian Cosmology.* Grand Rapids: Eerdmans, 2009.

Flynn, Gabriel, and Paul D. Murray, eds. *Ressourcement: A Movement for Renewal in Twentieth-Century Catholic Theology.* Oxford: Oxford University Press, 2012.

Francis I, Pope. *Laudato Si': On Care for Our Common Home.* Boston: Pauline, 2015.

Goldberg, David J., and John D. Rayner. *The Jewish People: Their History and Their Religion.* London: Penguin, 1987.

Gorman, Michael J. *Inhabiting the Cruciform God: Kenosis, Justification, and Theosis in Paul's Narrative Soteriology.* Grand Rapids: Eerdmans, 2009.

———. *Reading Paul.* Cascade Companions. Eugene, OR: Cascade, 2008.

Gregory of Nazianzus. *On God and Christ: The Five Theological Orations and Two Letters to Cledonius.* Translated Frederick Williams and Lionel Wickham. Crestwood, NY: St. Vladimir's Seminary Press, 2002.

Gregory of Nyssa. *The Life of Moses.* Translated by Everett Ferguson and Abraham Malherbe. Mahwah, NJ: Paulist, 1978.

———. *The Lord's Prayer and The Beatitudes.* Translated by Hilda Graef. Mahwah, NJ: Paulist, 1954.

Guerra, Marc D., ed. *Liberating Logos: Pope Benedict XVI's September Speeches.* South Bend, IN: St. Augustine's, 2014.

Hahn, Scott. *Covenant and Communion: The Biblical Theology of Pope Benedict XVI.* Grand Rapids: Brazos, 2009.

Hart, David Bentley. *That All Shall Be Saved: Heaven, Hell, and Universal Salvation.* New Haven: Yale University Press, 2019.

Hart, Trevor. *Between the Image and the Word: Theological Engagements with Imagination, Language, and Literature.* Burlington, VT: Ashgate, 2013.

Hays, Richard B. *Reading Backwards: Figural Christology and the Fourfold Gospel Witness.* Waco, TX: Baylor University Press, 2014.

Healy, Nicholas J. *The Eschatology of Hans Urs von Balthasar: Being in Communion.* Oxford: Oxford University Press, 2007.

Howsare, Rodney A. *Balthasar: A Guide for the Perplexed.* London: T. & T. Clark, 2009.

John Paul II, Pope. *Man and Woman He Created Them: A Theology of the Body.* Edited by M. Waldstein. Boston: Pauline, 2006.

———. *Ut Unum Sint: On Commitment to Ecumenism.* Boston: Pauline, 1995.

Jurgens, Willam A., ed. *The Faith of the Early Fathers.* Collegeville, MN: Liturgical, 1970.

Keating, Daniel. *Deification and Grace.* Naples, FL: Sapientia, 2007.

Keating, James, and Thomas J. White, eds. *Divine Impassibility and the Mystery of Human Suffering.* Grand Rapids: Eerdmans, 2009.

Keating, Thomas. *The Better Part: Stages of Contemplative Living.* New York: Continuum, 2000.

————. *Crisis of Faith, Crisis of Love*. New York: Continuum, 2009.

Kelly, Anthony J. *Upwards: Faith, Church, and the Ascension of Christ*. Collegeville, MN: Liturgical, 2014.

Knight, Douglas H. *The Eschatological Economy: Time and the Hospitality of God*. Grand Rapids: Eerdmans, 2006.

————. *The Theology of John Zizioulas: Personhood and the Church*. Burlington, VT: Ashgate, 2007.

Kreeft, Peter. *The Platonic Tradition*. South Bend, IN: St. Augustine's, 2018.

Krill, Philip. *Aporiae: Inquiries from the Eschaton*. Bloomington, IN: Author House, 2023.

————. *Le Point Vierge: Meditations on the Mystery of Presence*. Bloomington, IN: Author House, 2021.

Krill, Philip, and James McCullough. *Life in the Trinity: The Mystery of God and Human Deification*. Eugene, OR: Wipf & Stock, 2022.

Loder, James E. *The Logic of the Spirit: Human Development in Theological Perspective*. San Francisco: Jossey-Bass, 1998.

Louth, Andrew. *The Origins of the Christian Mystical Tradition*. Oxford: Clarendon, 1981.

Lubac, Henri de. *Corpus Mysticum: The Eucharist and the Church in the Middle Ages*. Translated Gemma Simmonds. London: SCM, 2006.

————. *History and Spirit: The Understanding of Scripture According to Origen*. Translated Anne England Nash. San Francisco: Ignatius, 2007.

————. *Medieval Exegesis, Vol. I: The Four Senses of Scripture*. Translated by Mark Sebanc. Grand Rapids: Eerdmans, 1998.

————. *Medieval Exegesis, Vol. II: The Four Senses of Scripture*. Translated by E. M. Macierowski. Grand Rapids: Eerdmans, 2000.

————. *Medieval Exegesis, Vol. III: The Four Senses of Scripture*. Translated by E. M. Macierowski. Grand Rapids: Eerdmans, 2009.

Maloney, George A. *Abiding in the Indwelling Trinity*. Mahwah, NJ: Paulist, 2004.

Manoussakis, John Panteleimon. *God After Metaphysics*. Bloomington: Indiana University Press, 2007.

Marion, Jean-Luc. *God Without Being*. Chicago: University of Chicago Press, 1991.

Martin, Ralph. *The Fulfillment of All Desire: A Guidebook for the Journey to God Based on the Wisdom of the Saints*. Steubenville, OH: Emmaus Road, 2006.

Maximus the Confessor. *Selected Writings*. Edited by G. Berthold. Mahwah, NJ: Paulist, 1985.

Mazza, Enrico. *Mystagogy*. New York: Pueblo, 1989.

McCullough, James. *Sense and Spirituality: The Arts and Spiritual Formation*. Eugene, OR: Cascade, 2015.

McIntosh, Mark A. *Christology from Within: Spirituality and the Incarnation in Hans Urs von Balthasar*. Notre Dame: University of Notre Dame Press, 2000.

McPartlan, Paul. *The Eucharist Makes the Church: Henri de Lubac and John Zizioulas in Dialogue*. Fairfax, VA: Eastern Christian, 2006.

———. *Sacrament of Salvation: An Introduction to Eucharistic Ecclesiology*. Edinburgh: T. & T. Clark, 1995.

Mongrain, Kevin. *The Systematic Thought of Hans Urs von Balthasar: An Irenaean Retrieval*. New York: Crossroads, 2002.

Neder, Adam. *Participation in Christ: An Entry into Karl Barth's Church Dogmatics*. Louisville: Westminster John Knox, 2009.

Niebuhr, H. Richard. *Christ and Culture*. 50th Anniversary ed. San Francisco: HarperCollins, 2001.

Nouwen, Henri. *Behold the Beauty of the Lord: Praying with Icons*. Notre Dame: Ave Maria, 1987.

O'Donnell, John. *Hans Urs von Balthasar*. London: Chapman, 1992.

———. "Hans Urs von Balthasar: The Form of His Theology." *Communio* 16 (1989) 458–74.

O'Hanlon, G. F. *The Immutability of God in the Theology of Hans Urs von Balthasar*. New York: Cambridge University Press, 1990.

O'Keefe, John J., and R. R. Reno. *Sanctified Vision: An Introduction to Early Christian Interpretation of the Bible*. Baltimore: Johns Hopkins University Press, 2005.

Paul VI, Pope. *Pastoral Constitution on the Church in the Modern World (Gaudium et Spes)*. St. Louis: Pauline Books and Media, 1965.

Penna, Romano. *Paul the Apostle: Wisdom and Folly of the Cross*. Collegeville, MN: Liturgical, 1996.

Pontifical Biblical Commission. *The Interpretation of the Bible in the Church*. Boston: St. Paul, 1993.

———. *The Jewish People and Their Scriptures in the Christian Bible*. Vatican City: Libreria Editrice Vaticana, 2002.

Principe, Walter. "Towards Defining Spirituality." *Sciences Religieuses/Studies in Religion* 12 (1983) 127–41.

Pseudo-Dionysius. *The Complete Works*. Translated by Colm Luibheid. Mahwah, NJ: Paulist, 1987.

Rahner, Karl. *The Trinity*. New York: Crossroad, 1997.

Ramelli, Ilaria E. *A Larger Hope? Universal Salvation from Christian Beginnings to Julian of Norwich*. Eugene, OR: Cascade, 2019.

Ratzinger, Joseph. *Behold the Pierced One: An Approach to a Spiritual Christology*. San Francisco: Ignatius, 1986.

———. *Called to Communion: Understanding the Church Today*. San Francisco: Ignatius, 1996.

———. "Concerning the Notion of Person in Theology." *Communio* 17 (1990) 439–54.

———. *The Feast of Faith: Approaches to a Theology of the Liturgy*. Translated by Graham Harrison. San Francisco: Ignatius, 1986.

———. *Introduction to Christianity*. San Francisco: Ignatius, 1990.

———. *On the Way to Jesus Christ*. San Francisco: Ignatius, 2020.

———. *Principals of Catholic Theology*. San Francisco: Ignatius, 1987.

————. *The Yes of Jesus Christ*. New York: Crossroad, 1991.

Richardson, Cyril C., ed. *Early Christian Fathers*. New York: Collier, 1970.

Rohr, Richard. *The Divine Dance: The Trinity and Your Transformation*. New Kensington, PA: Whitaker House, 2016.

————. *Falling Upwards: A Spirituality of the Two Halves of Life*. San Francisco: Jossey-Bass, 2011.

Rowland, Tracey. *Ratzinger's Faith: The Theology of Pope Benedict XVI*. Oxford: Oxford University Press, 2008.

Russell, Norman. *The Doctrine of Deification in the Greek Patristic Tradition*. Oxford: Oxford University Press, 2004.

Shea, Mark P. *Making Senses Out of Scripture: Reading the Bible as the First Christians Did*. Bucharest: Basilica, 2016.

Schindler, D. C. "The Redemption of Eros: Philosophical Reflections on Benedict XVI's First Encyclical." *Communio* 33 (2006) 375–400.

Schmemann, Alexander. *For the Life of the World: Sacraments and Orthodoxy*. Crestwood, NY: St. Vladimir's Seminary Press, 1973.

Schönborn, Christoph. *From Death to Life: The Christian Journey*. San Francisco: Ignatius, 1995.

————. *God Sent His Son: A Contemporary Christology*. San Francisco: Ignatius, 2010.

————. *God's Human Face: The Christ-Icon*. San Francisco: Ignatius, 1994.

Schumacher, Michelle M. *A Trinitarian Anthropology: Adrienne von Speyr and Hans Urs von Balthasar in Dialogue with Thomas Aquinas*. Washington, DC: The Catholic University of America Press, 2015.

Shults, F. LeRon, and Steven J. Sandage. *Transforming Spirituality: Integrating Theology and Psychology*. Grand Rapids: Baker Academic, 2006.

Sire, James W. *Naming the Elephant: Worldview as a Concept*. Downers Grove, IL: InterVarsity, 2004.

Smith, Christian, and Melinda Lundquist Denton. *Soul Searching: The Religious and Spiritual Lives of American Teenagers*. Oxford: Oxford University Press, 2005.

Steenberg, M. C. *Of God and Man: Theology as Anthropology from Irenaeus to Athanasius*. London: T. & T. Clark, 2009.

Symeon the New Theologian. *Divine Eros: Hymns of Saint Symeon the New Theologian*. Translated by By Daniel K. Griggs. Crestwood, NY: St. Vladimir's Seminary Press, 2010.

Tanner, Kathryn. *Jesus, Humanity, and the Trinity: A Brief Systematic Theology*. Minneapolis: Fortress, 2001.

Tanner, Norman P., ed. *Decrees of the Ecumenical Councils*. 2 vols. Washington, DC: Georgetown University Press, 1990.

Thunberg, Lars. *Man and Cosmos: The Theological Anthropology of Maximus the Confessor*. Crestwood, NY: St. Vladimir's Seminary Press, 1985.

Tracy, David. *The Analogical Imagination: Christian Theology and the Culture of Pluralism*. New York: Crossroads, 1981.

Volf, Miroslav. *After Our Likeness: The Church as the Image of the Trinity*. Grand Rapids: Eerdmans, 1998.

Ward, Benedicta, trans. *The Desert Fathers: Sayings of the Early Christian Monks*. London: Penguin, 2003.

Weinandy, Thomas G. *Does God Suffer?* Notre Dame: University of Notre Dame Press, 2000.

Wilken, Robert Louis. *The Spirit of Early Christian Thought: Seeking the Face of God*. New Haven: Yale University Press, 2003.

Wood, Susan K. *Spiritual Exegesis and the Church in the Theology of Henri de Lubac*. Grand Rapids: Eerdmans, 1998.

Zizioulas, John. *Being as Communion: Studies in Personhood and the Church*. Crestwood, NY: St. Vladimir Seminary Press, 1985.

———. *The Meaning of Being Human*. Alhambra, CA: Sebastian, 2021.

Index

www.ingramcontent.com/pod-product-compliance
Lightning Source LLC
Chambersburg PA
CBHW032234080426
42735CB00008B/843